Studies in German Literature, Linguistics, and Culture:
Literary Criticism in Perspective

Nestroy and the Critics

Nestroy and the Critics

Caricature of Nestroy published in 1842 as the frontispiece to Friedrich Kaiser's play "Wer wird Amtmann?" Nestroy is shown in the main role, that of Florian Baumlang

W. E. Yates

Nestroy and the Critics

CAMDEN HOUSE

Published by Camden House, Inc.
Drawer 2025
Columbia, SC 29202 USA

Printed on acid-free paper.
Binding materials are chosen for strength and
durability.

ISBN:1-879751-97-6

Library of Congress Cataloging-in-Publication Data

Yates, W. E.
    Nestroy and the critics / W.E. Yates.
        p.   cm. — (Studies in German literature, linguistics, and culture. Literary
criticism in perspective)
    Includes bibliographical references and index.
    ISBN 1-879751-97-6 (alk. paper)
    1. Nestroy, Johann, 1801-1862—Criticism and interpretation.
    I. Title. II. Series.
    PT2440.N3Z94
    832'.7—dc20   94-4384
                                                                      CIP

Acknowledgments

The community of Nestroy scholars is a very friendly one, and I am grateful for countless pieces of advice and acts of support. In particular my warm thanks are due to Walter Obermaier, Louise Adey Huish, Christel Thomsen, Friedrich Walla, John R. P. McKenzie, and most especially Jürgen Hein for supplying me with otherwise inaccessible material; also to Karl Zimmel, Friedrich Walla, and Jürgen Hein for some invaluable bibliographical tips.

It is as always a pleasure to record my grateful dependence on the resources of the Wiener Stadt- und Landesbibliothek, and the helpfulness of its staff; and I must also express my thanks to the staff of the other libraries I have used in working on this volume, in particular the Österreichische Nationalbibliothek (whose theater collection has since 1991 been held in the Österreichisches Theatermuseum); Exeter University Library; and the Institute of Germanic Studies, University of London. I should also record that the book draws substantially on work I did less recently in the Cambridge University Library and the Deutsches Literaturarchiv in Marbach.

I must also thank the series editors James Hardin and Eitel Timm for their watchful encouragement, and James Hardin for his patience, kindness, and help in dealing with my computer text. I also have to thank my colleague Lesley Sharpe for her careful reading of a typescript draft. Finally I owe a special debt of gratitude to John McKenzie, who also read a draft of my text and has helped me with many knowledgeable comments.

W. E. Y.

Contents

Preface   xi

1:Nestroy's Controversial Career in the Theater   1

2:The Image of Cynicism   12

3:The Nestroy Renaissance   24

4:The Postwar Boom   36

     a: The Establishment of a "Classic"   36

     b: The Major Advances   46

5:Edition and Discovery   56

6: Cruxes of Modern Criticism   62

Bibliography   73

Index   105

Preface

All history of reception, such as the series *Literary Criticism in Perspective* sets out to chart, reflects movements in opinion and taste which are determined by the ever-changing Zeitgeist. To that extent, the history of critical interpretation tends to follow a similar pattern for most authors. Nestroy's reputation too has been subject to the vagaries both of taste and of ideology. But his case is particularly complicated, in ways that derive directly from the fact that he was an actor-dramatist, who as an actor enjoyed popularity with theater audiences but whose work both as an actor and as a playwright was from the first viewed with suspicion by conservative critics.

Consequently the history of his critical reception needs to be viewed on two levels. His standing with the general public, as we can trace it through the growth of a Nestroy "image," has never been the same as his standing in more specialist criticism. Moreover, the critics were for a long time unable to base their assessment on printed texts of any but a few plays; indeed, the first full edition to provide a text matching up to scholarly standards is still incomplete. The historical shortage of authorized published texts makes the position quite different from that we face when tracing the reception of, say, a novelist, even a novelist whose reputation has been controversial. The story I have to unfold is not just one of vagaries in interpretation and evaluation but of a struggle towards any kind of serious understanding; this is linked to the late development of serious Nestroy scholarship.

The interpretative literature on Nestroy is still patchy. If one conclusion to be drawn from the history of Nestroy criticism is that it has been depressingly slow to come of age, another is much more encouraging, namely that there are still abundant openings for work on him, based on the full range of documentation which has gradually become available.

Quantitatively, however, there is an enormous amount of Nestroy criticism. The problematical character of his reception means that some of the most revealing material is not in monographs and learned articles but in press appreciations, including theater reviews. Like many playwrights working for the commercial theater, he was a prolific writer, despite the extremely heavy load he carried as the leading popular actor of mid-nineteenth-century Vienna. He wrote over eighty plays. (That may seem an unsatisfactorily imprecise statement, but as they are nearly all adapted from borrowed material, there is some dispute in a few cases about the authenticity of his authorship.) Of the plays performed in Vienna, there are on average at least six reviews for each première, and more for revivals. There are reviews of his performances outside Vienna, and reviews of productions outside Vienna in which he was not involved. There are obituaries. There are reviews of productions since his death — hundreds of productions, indeed: for a time during the 1960s and 1970s he was one of the half-dozen most performed playwrights in the German-speaking theater. There are articles commemorating anniversaries, from 1912 (a turning-point in his reputation) onwards. And especially in the last thirty years or so there has been a large output of academic criticism.

Therefore I have to begin with an apology. The names of many critics and scholars who have published on Nestroy do not appear at all in my bibliography (which is arranged chronologically); others are represented only by a small proportion of their published work. Many will be disappointed that I have proceeded so selectively. But there is always a danger in surveys of criticism that they can degenerate into lists; I have tried to concentrate on significant developments, and to pick out representative examples at each stage of the story. Fuller bibliographical guidance can be found in the surveys of Nestroy scholarship by Jürgen Hein, to which I refer at appropriate points.

1: Nestroy's Controversial Career in the Theater

The German-speaking theater boasts a long and lively tradition of comedy. That is not how it is usually thought of elsewhere; it has an unenviable image as an institution of solemnity and high moral seriousness. The discrepancy has a historical explanation: it derives from the long-standing contrast between the court theaters (later national and state theaters), which were subsidized to foster serious drama, and independent acting companies, from the strolling players of the seventeenth century to the commercial theaters of the nineteenth-century cities. The literary pretensions of the court and national theaters established the critical expectations of generations of moralistic and conservative reviewers; this meant that for an actor-dramatist such as Johann Nepomuk Nestroy, writing dialect comedies spiced with musical numbers, recognition by heavy-weight critics was inevitably an uphill struggle, despite (or even as a consequence of) his successes at the box-office. Nestroy was stamped as the irreverent darling of the uncritical public of Biedermeier Vienna — an audience that Karl Gutzkow, for example, described in 1845 as pouring into the theaters, fascinated by every new play, and applauding with undiscriminating enthusiasm (Gutzkow 1845: 293). This popularity, bordering on idolatry, is reflected in the report of his funeral which appeared in *The Times* on 10 June 1862:

> ... Nestroy, a renowned dramatic author and comedian, who for 30 years was one of the idols of this city, is dead and buried. It is said, and I believe without exaggeration, that between 40,000 and 50,000 persons were assembled in the streets through which the coffin containing the mortal remains of the Austrian Aristophanes were carried. (Anon. 1862)

The label "Austrian Aristophanes" was to become a cliché as Nestroy's career passed into legend. Of course, show-business always spawns legends; but nowhere more so than in Vienna, where the theater has long occupied a central place in cultural and social life. Born in 1801, Nestroy succeeded Ferdinand Raimund (1790-1836) in the early 1830s as the most popular Viennese actor-dramatist; over the next thirty years nearly all his plays were given their first performance in Vienna with Nestroy himself in a leading role. (Many were subsequently performed in other towns, especially in the far-flung Austrian provinces.) At the beginning of his career he took over the *Zauberspiel* genre used by Raimund but abandoned it in the mid-1830s, gradually working his way to the form of *Posse mit Gesang* (literally, "farce with singing") characteristic of his mature work; the decisive turning-point may be seen in *Glück, Mißbrauch und Rückkehr* of 1838 (see Yates 1988a: 103), and the period of his greatest mastery is generally regarded as having lain in the early 1840s.

The term *Posse* gave rise to numerous problems. Nestroy uses all the devices of farcical comedy, but his best plays have a reflective and specifically satirical force which stands in sharp contrast to the vacuity of farce. This was often acknowledged by reviewers. Moritz Saphir (1795-1858), for example, reviewing *Zu ebener Erde und erster Stock*, asked why Nestroy had called it a *Lokalposse*, a term that implied a limited appeal (Saphir 1835: 779). Two years later another critic, reviewing *Das Haus der Temperamente*, suggested that the gulf between Nestroy and the other Viennese dialect dramatists was so enormous that he ought to find a more appropriate term than "Posse" (ch l————— 1837: 683). (Many critics signed their reviews with ciphers; "ch l—————" was a regular contributor to *Der Humorist*.) In 1846 and 1847 Nestroy's choice of the term "Posse" for *Der Unbedeutende* and *Der Schützling* was called into question in the Viennese journals (Adami 1846; Norbert 1847: 387; Arnold 1847b: 366); and reviewing the first Prague production of *Der Schützling*, Bernhard Gutt (1812-49) also judged that the play was not a true *Posse* ("eigentlich keine Posse") and suggested that it was rather "a drama with elements of comedy and occasionally in the style of farce" ("ein Schauspiel mit einzelnen Lustspielelementen und hin und wieder dem Style der Posse") (Gutt 1847a).

This is only a small part of the critical disagreement Nestroy's plays provoked. Their reception was chequered at almost every stage of his career, which was rich in controversy. Some of his unexpected flops may have been the consequence of interventions by the censor; this may, for example, have been the case with the satire *Eine Wohnung ist zu vermieten*, which was hissed off the stage in 1837 (see Yates 1985b: 62). But popular legend simplifies the picture, in one of two ways. In his own time, and indeed until the end of the nineteenth century, Nestroy was often regarded as a dangerous "cynic"; as that charge has lost conviction, he has tended to be thought of, especially outside Austria, as part of an innocent theatrical idyll associated with "Old Vienna," as the author of a succession of uncomplicated farces, light-heartedly witty where Raimund's had been sentimental, and sometimes spiced in performance with daring extempores.

In the words of the refrain of one of Nestroy's best-known satirical songs, "'s ist alles nit wahr" (*SW* 4: 77-80). The much-admired lightness of his writing was a hard-won quality, honed by revision, but critics in his own time repeatedly assumed, wrongly, that for all his undeniable "genius" he wrote without care (see Yates 1991a); the more entertaining a work, the more likely a critic was to assume that it was something that had been dashed off quickly ("eine flüchtige Arbeit"), as one reviewer of *Einen Jux will er sich machen* did in 1842 (————e 1842). Franz von Dingelstedt, writing in the same year in the *Wiener Zeitschrift für Kunst, Literatur, Theater und Mode* (of all the Viennese journals the one with the most serious literary pretensions), also took it for granted that Nestroy often worked too rapidly and carelessly ("zu geschwind und zu leichtfertig") in adapting his sources (Dingelstedt 1842), and three years later another critic attributed the failure of *Das Gewürzkrämer-Kleeblatt* to the speed of its composition (Markbreiter 1845: 134). As a working dramatist providing material for a commercial theater Nestroy certainly wrote at speed, but what he wrote was material for performance by himself, and from his manuscripts it is clear that he polished it with great care.

There were always external factors to be taken into consideration: he had to fight an endless battle to outwit the vigilance of the censor, and he was also constantly subject to the pressures of reception by a rapidly changing theater public and a largely hostile press, which there is no doubt he read attentively (see Obermaier 1991).

When surveying the reviews he received during his lifetime, one needs to distinguish, as far as it is possible to do so, between the critics' judgments of his plays and their response to his acting. This is often difficult because the critics tended to blur the distinction; indeed, even so shrewd a critic as Ludwig Speidel (1830-1906), who was in Vienna from 1853 onwards, insisted that in Nestroy's case it was "impossible to separate author and performer" (Speidel 1888: 399). His *acting* style from his early years on seems to have been based on aggressive caricature, which struck contemporary observers, by comparison with previous (more sentimental) comic actors, as bringing a challenging reflection of real life into the popular dialect theater; in fact it involved not realism but comic exaggeration supporting specifically satirical effects (see Rommel 1930: 181-82; Mautner 1937: 8). The comic power of his acting was universally acknowledged; the Viennese papers carried innumerable general statements about the irresistible effect of his performances, especially in tandem with Wenzel Scholz (1787-1857). Their standing may be gauged by the fact that when no less a judge than Grillparzer arrived in Hamburg on 18 September 1847 with his traveling companion, Wilhelm Bogner, and heard that Nestroy and Scholz were appearing at the Thalia-Theater, their reaction, as recorded in Bogner's diary of their journey, was to go there on their very first evening, despite the effects of their long and tiring journey from Leipzig, in the hope of seeing the two actors on stage. (In vain; their performances in Hamburg were already over.)

The most searching analyses of Nestroy's acting style were, in fact, written about his performances on tour in the mid-1840s, and stem from two reviewers publishing in the Prague daily *Bohemia*. Nestroy first appeared in Prague in 1840, and was reviewed in *Bohemia* by Anton Müller (1792-1843), who was struck by a strong element of caricature in his acting (see Theobald 1992). A similar impression was recorded five years later when he appeared in *Der Zerrissene* in Frankfurt (W. 1847), and it remained the impression he made, including in his delivery, to the end of his life: in his last appearances in Vienna he still seemed "the very embodiment of caricature from head to toe" ("vom Scheitel bis zur Sohle die lebendige Carricatur" [Silberstein 1861]). In 1842, when he returned to Prague for his third visit and appeared in *Einen Jux will er sich machen,* Müller, by now an enthusiastic admirer, reviewed him again. After Müller's death the theater reviewing in *Bohemia* was taken over by Gutt; long extracts from his accounts in 1844 were reprinted in *Die Fackel* in 1924 (Kraus 1924) and were quickly recognized as the most authoritative analysis by an eye-witness. Gutt observed a more benignly humorous quality in Nestroy's performing style than there had been in the grotesque effects of earlier years.

Throughout his career, Nestroy was celebrated for his solo scenes. In his monologues he displayed a distinctive bravura of delivery (see Schlögl 1883: 150), while the satirical songs (*Couplets*) were always regarded as an essential ingredient of his best plays, "die Forcebeigabe Nestroys" (Wiest 1837: 365). This was no doubt partly a tribute to his skill as a singer (he had begun his theatrical career as an operatic bass). In the early 1840s, when he reduced the quantity of musical numbers in his plays in order to achieve a more concentrated satirical effect (see Branscombe 1971-72: 108-9; Hein 1986: 114-15), this did not pass without critical complaints (e.g. Lewinsky 1842). But the effect of the songs in perform-ance remained one of the strengths of almost every new Nestroy production. A typical reaction is that of Gutt, reviewing Nestroy's fourth appearance in *Der Schützling* in Prague in 1847 (his hundredth appearance altogether in Prague): Gutt reported that the climax of the play's polemical effect lay in the *Couplet* in the fourth act, and indeed that these particular satirical verses were the best he had ever heard (Gutt 1847b).

On the aesthetic and even moral effects of his acting, opinion was quickly divided. He did not idealize; and while on the one hand there were those who stressed the impression of "truthfulness" ("Wahrheit") he conveyed (e.g. Weid-mann 1834), on the other hand he was also accused of coarseness, especially in his use of indecent gestures and facial expressions. Certainly the expressiveness of his gestures was a much-attested feature of his performance. Accounts twenty years apart describe the combination of lively mime and ironic expression in his "excellent" acting ("das ausgezeichnete Spiel dieses Künstlers, in welchem jede Bewegung drastisch, jeder Blick Ironie ist" [Naske 1841: 1135]), his "agile hands and legs", ("mit seinen agilen Händen und Beinen"), and his "unique gift of indicating intellectual superiority by a single twitch of the eyes of lips" ("eine merkwürdige unerreichte Gabe: durch eine einzige Mundfalte, ein einziges Augenzucken die ganze geistige ironische Höhe neben der scheinbar tiefst-dümmsten Rede anzudeuten" [Silberstein 1861]). What was insistently held against him was the use he put this gift to. In 1847, for example, a critic discussing what he saw as the prevalent obscenity of acting in the dialect theater ("die Zotenreißerei der Schauspieler"), described how the actors got round the censors' watchfulness by suggestive gesture and in so doing alienated the more educated section of the theater public (Arnold 1847a: 302). From the two specific examples he cites, *Zwölf Mädchen in Uniform* and Louis Grois's *Eine Dorfgeschichte, die in der Stadt endet*, it is clear that his principal target is Nestroy, who played the main part in both.

Critical complaints about the suggestiveness actors achieved by means of gesture had been common long before Nestroy (see Walla 1991: 247); what is important in Nestroy's case is that the charge was extended to his plays, whose supposed indecency was often said to detract from their wit (e.g. Viola 1841: 1441). His sceptical view of the world led frequently to criticisms that in characterization and language his work was coarse; it was too concerned with low life, was marred by vulgar crudity ("Derbheit"), and offered no edifying moral teaching. Among the prominent regular reviewers, Saphir, who became the editor of *Der Humorist* in 1837, repeatedly voiced such criticisms (see Rommel 1930: 581). Both he and Ludwig August Frankl (1810-94) compared Nestroy with Dickens in respect of what they perceived as his harshly uncompromising realism: Frankl called him the "Boz" of the German stage ("Nestroy ist der deutsche Boz auf den Brettern"), Saphir called him the "Boz" of the popular theater, an unsentimental realist whose characters were drawn from the real world of the streets and taverns, but who shared with Dickens a preference for the seamier side of human nature (Frankl 1842: 58; Saphir 1843: 931-32); and he accused Nestroy of corrupting taste, especially by establishing an expectation of indecency (Saphir 1842: 207). To modern eyes the charge of indecency seems incomprehensible, unfounded in his texts. But even if we allow for changes in taste and in moral standards, there clearly must have been a discrepancy between the words spoken, which had been prepared for scrutiny by the censor or his representatives at performances, and the manner in which they were delivered, outwitting official vigilance; in this there was doubtless an element of "liberating" compensation for the impossibility of commenting openly on matters of public concern (see Speidel 1881: 2; Matt 1976: 8; Häusler 1987: 72-74).

There is also abundant evidence from contemporary observers confirming that in his own time, in particular by comparison with Raimund, the aggressiveness and disrespectfulness that Nestroy suggested by his acting seemed to belong to a new era and had an unsettling effect; hence, no doubt, the nervousness of conservative critics about what they thought was his corrupting social influence. Contemporaries, both inside and outside Vienna, genuinely found the contrast between Nestroy's plays and Raimund's stark and shocking (see Theobald 1993). The sense of implicit threat in his style of performance was expressed most unambiguously by a Burgtheater actor, Carl Ludwig Costenoble (1769-1837). After watching him in a comedy by a minor contemporary playwright, Friedrich Hopp (1789-1869), Costenoble wrote that the effect Nestroy projected was always reminiscent of the "dregs of the mob" who were ready to indulge in plundering and murder when revolution came. However comic Nestroy was at times, so Costenoble's note continues, he could not prevent an eerie sense of threat from coming over spectators:

> Sein Wesen ... erinnert immer an diejenige Hefe des Pöbels, die in Revolutionsfällen zum Plündern und Todschlagen bereit ist. Wie komisch Nestroy auch zuweilen wird — er kann das Unheimliche nicht verdrängen, welches den Zuhörer beschleicht. (Costenoble 1837: 336)

Julius Seidlitz (1814-57) published a scathing attack on the demeaning crudeness, as he saw it, of *Lumpacivagabundus* and on the decline of the moral tone of the dialect stage by comparison with the heyday of Raimund and Adolf Bäuerle (1786-1859) in the 1820s (Seidlitz 1837: 1: 182-88). In the same year the failure in performance of *Eine Wohnung ist zu vermieten* provided an opportunity for the critics to give full reign to their hostility. Though there were at that time seven or eight Viennese journals that appeared several times a week (or at least weekly) and gave a lot of space to detailed discussion of new theatrical productions, there were no critics in Vienna of the same calibre as Théophile Gautier in Paris. Gautier had a lively understanding of the expectations it was appropriate to have of a light musical comedy (*comédie-vaudeville*); in Vienna, by contrast, the standards of the reviewers were rooted in aesthetic norms derived from the eighteenth century. Suspicious of satire as lacking "pathos," many of them adhered to a conception of the theater as a "moral institution," and maintained that popular comedy in particular should have an improving function, so that a play such as *Glück, Mißbrauch und Rückkehr*, which could be read as having a sound moral, was praised as a step in the right direction, an attempt to "emancipate" local drama from a "morass of obscenity" ("die Localmuse von dem Schlamme der Gemeinheit zu emancipiren" [Tuvora 1838]).

The prevalent moralism repeatedly hampered the critics' capacity to appreciate the essential function of comedy as enjoyable entertainment. They had one of the great masters of European comedy in their midst, and could not bring themselves to acknowledge this without grudging qualifications. In particular they often had an ambivalent attitude towards the virtuosity of Nestroy's wordplay. Even Gutt, who wrote perceptively about Nestroy's technique as a dramatist, and who anticipated modern criticism in recognizing a Baroque quality in his linguistic inventiveness and vivid imagery, put this negatively when reviewing *Der Schützling*, in which he judged that the lavishness of the wordplay seemed coldly artificial and over-florid: "Es ist in diesem Schwulst von Witz etwas Hofmannswaldauisches" (Gutt 1847a). In Vienna, the reviewers' obsessive criticism of what they regarded as the trivial character of his wit often blinded them to the scope of his satire. One example is the criticism by Emanuel Straube (1801-72) of the lack of a positive moral (a "sühnende Moral") in *Einen Jux will er sich machen* and his reservations about the role of "chance" in a plot skilfully and deliberately constructed out of a hilarious sequence of coincidences (Straube 1842). Critics in the vanguard of this moral concern included those writing, like Straube, for the *Wiener Zeitschrift für Kunst, Literatur, Theater und Mode*, which was edited from 1836 to 1844 by Friedrich Witthauer (d. 1846) and which adhered to firmly moralistic criteria, seeing all drama as having a didactic purpose.

Judged by such criteria, the development of dialect comedy in Nestroy's time by comparison with the more sentimental and much less satirical comedy of the 1820s was a bad thing, and by the late 1830s laments about the decline of dialect comedy (e.g. Schmidt 1838) were frequent. Criticism was sharpened when in December 1838 Karl Carl (1787-1854), the shrewd director of the Theater an der Wien, where Nestroy and Scholz worked, took over the Theater in der Leopoldstadt also. This theater was the traditional home of dialect comedy, where most of Raimund's career had been spent, and Carl's takeover seemed to signal the passing of an era. By the end of the decade it was widely accepted that the popular theater was in decline. Even Raimund was occasionally blamed for having contributed to the changed complexion of the popular stage (Saphir 1835: 779; Wagner 1843b: 1094), and this view continued to be voiced, as for example by Bauernfeld, giving an account of the "undeniable" decline of the popular stage in the early 1850s (Bauernfeld 1853: 100-1). More commonly, however, Raimund was regarded as a model — an actor-dramatist whose work had been carefully written, had evoked tears as well as laughter, and had been informed by a healthy moralistic intention. The cliché of the contrast between the idealistic Raimund and the critical Nestroy did not develop only after Nestroy's death (*pace* Hein 1990: 125) but was already well established by 1840.

By the same token, critics praised any sign that as well as merely working to amuse, Nestroy was moving towards appealing to the "heart": part of the praise lavished on *Glück, Mißbrauch und Rückkehr*, for example, was because at least some scenes achieved not just belly-laughs but "feeling" ("doch wirken die Szenen hier und da nicht bloß auf das Zwerchfell, sondern auch auf das Gemüth" [Gross-Hoffinger 1838]). Saphir similarly praised *Die verhängnisvolle Faschingsnacht* as evidence of Nestroy's ability "das Herz und das Zwerchfell zu erschüttern" (Saphir 1839: 303). When the new Carltheater, built on the site of the Theater in der Leopoldstadt, opened in 1847, Saphir used the occasion as an opportunity for further discussion of the decline of popular theater since Raimund's death. Though Nestroy had more genius than Raimund, so Saphir argued, he lacked Raimund's moral idealism; though he was wittier than Raimund, his wit was only an end in itself: "Es fehlt ihm durchaus der Glaube an [die] Existenz einer höhern Idee und eines sittlichen Ideals. ... Bei Raimund war der Witz das Mittel, bei Nestroy ist er *Zweck*." In this, according to Saphir, Nestroy showed similarities to Bauernfeld, who was writing salon comedies for the Burgtheater at the time (Saphir 1847b: 1198).

Throughout the 1840s Nestroy was at the centre of sustained controversy. It was a time of rapid social change in Vienna: the population was expanding rapidly, and social and political tensions were building up which would eventually erupt in the revolution of 1848. In this climate critics of conservative persuasion both in matters of aesthetics and in politics pressed from the late 1830s onwards for a new kind of play, to which the specific term *Volksstück* was applied. (It was only later that the term came to be attached to all popular dialect drama.) The new kind of play being demanded should be not "witty" but rather "humorous" in tone (the term implies a considerable degree of sentimentality), should teach an edifying moral, and should present an idealized view of everyday life (see Yates 1985a, 1987; Hein 1989b). Its most vocal champion was Saphir; he recognized the strength of Nestroy's satire but even when he acknowledged Nestroy's "colossal wit," the phrase "kolossaler Witz" is not meant wholly as praise but stands in contrast to Raimund (Saphir 1847a: 467).

The controversy came to a head following the première in September 1840 of *Wer wird Amtmann?*, the play with which Friedrich Kaiser (1814-74) launched a sentimental genre which he called the "Lebensbild." The term, meaning "picture of life," implied a realistic intention, the presentation of life as it really was by contrast both with the triviality that Kaiser saw in contemporary comedy and with the distortion of which Nestroy constantly stood accused. *Wer wird Amtmann?* was praised for introducing precisely the new blend of sentiment and morality demanded by the supporters of the *Volksstück*. Nestroy had satirized the taste for sentimental "humor" rather than wit as early as 1833 in the figure of the soap-maker Blasius Grundl in *Weder Lorbeerbaum noch Bettelstab* (*SW* 3: 336-37); in *Der Talisman*, which was his next play after *Wer wird Amtmann?*, he included an open attack on Kaiser, a direct allusion to the *Lebensbild* genre, which Titus defines as a "sad farce" ("traurige Posse" [*HKA: Stücke 17/i*: 59]) — a phrase borrowed from an adverse review of one of Nestroy's own plays, *Gegen Torheit gibt es kein Mittel*, and now turned on his rival (see Yates 1978, 1991b). Significantly, most of the passage satirizing the *Lebensbild* was deleted by the censor (see *HKA: Stücke 17/i*: 325-26). There was no love lost between Nestroy and Kaiser, who as a critic had joined in the chorus of condemnation of *Eine Wohnung ist zu vermieten* (Kaiser 1837); and tensions developed within the theater, with the director, Karl Carl, insisting that his playwrights adhere to Nestroy's style (Kaiser 1854: 51-52). The dispute about the *Volksstück* is reflected in the critics' wish to find a term other than *Posse* for Nestroy's more weighty plays; in 1847 one term that was advanced as more appropriate for *Der Schützling*, in view of the preponderance of "serious" material, was none other than "Lebensbild" (Norbert 1847: 387; see Yates 1993b).

The misunderstandings that Nestroy encountered both in critics and, at least occasionally, in the theater public are classic examples of the pitfalls with which the satirist is perennially confronted. On the one hand, he was constrained to entertain the very public he was satirizing. As one modern commentator puts it, he was unlike his predecessors in that he "did not coddle the sensibilities of his bourgeois audience" (Corriher 1981: 27); hence some of the virulence in the rejection of *Eine Wohnung ist zu vermieten*, which not only failed to entertain as a comedy but whose satire struck home too harshly. On the other hand, the critics repeatedly confused the satirist with his subject, criticizing him for daring to present at all qualities in life (crudeness, pettiness, self-seeking, philistinism) that he was in fact presenting critically, which is the very business of satire. The answer lies in a speech of Salerl in *Zu ebener Erde und erster Stock* I,5: "One must take the world as it is, and not as it might be" ("Man muß die Welt nehmen, wie s' is, und nicht, wie s' sein könnt'" [*SW* 6: 19]); it is a distinction that the critics constantly failed to make.

What sharpened the critical controversy was the widespread realization that the whole future of Viennese popular theater lay in Nestroy's hands. This was because of his position as the outstanding dramatist in a period of "degeneration," the "Entartung unserer Volksbühne"; he was, as Schindler put it, the obvious defender of the *Lokalposse* and saviour of the popular stage (Schindler 1844: 11). That passage appeared in one of the most important dailies, the *Oesterreichisches Morgenblatt*, which was founded in 1836 and edited for a time by Ludwig August Frankl, then from mid-1841 by Johann Nepomuk Vogl (1802-66); its reviewers repeatedly measured Nestroy's achievement against the responsibility he had for the future of the popular theater. They did so either in hope — he alone was capable of propping up local comedy, which had "recently declined so grievously" ("Nestroy ist allein der Mann, der das in neuester Zeit so sehr in Verfall gekommene Feld der Lokalposse noch ein wenig aufrecht hält" [Schmidt 1838]) — or in disappointment: "We pinned our hope on Nestroy, trusting that in his latest play he would achieve a success that would be decisive for the future development of the dialect theater ("daß er mit seinem neuesten Stücke einen Wurf machen werde, der die Entscheidung sein soll für die künftige Richtung unserer Vorstadtbühne"); but our hopes have been dashed: Nestroy has failed" ("und siehe da, alles ist zu nichte geworden, Nestroy hat fallirt") (Schindler 1843). The weight of expectation placed on him meant that he was all the more vehemently attacked when he failed to fit in with fashionable demands and disappointed the critics by failing, as they saw it, to rise above the vapidity of the *Posse* (e.g. Wagner 1843a).

The *Oesterreichisches Morgenblatt*, on the other hand, defended the indigenous *Posse* (e.g. Nordmann 1843) and criticized Nestroy for not leading the resistance against the imported *comédie-vaudeville*, the "Genre ..., gegen das Nestroy die offenbare Opposition bilden sollte" (Schindler 1844: 11). Of the eleven full-length comedies by Nestroy that were premièred between December 1840 and Karl Carl's vacation of the Theater an der Wien in April 1845, at least seven were based on *comédies-vaudevilles*. These were *Der Talisman, Das Mädl aus der Vorstadt, Die Papiere des Teufels, Eisenbahnheiraten, Der Zerrissene, Das Gewürzkrämer-Kleeblatt*, and *Unverhofft*. (In one other, *Die beiden Herrn Söhne*, Nestroy also made use of at least one *comédie-vaudeville*.) One of the most consistent points in contemporary Nestroy criticism was a demand for "original" material rather than plots borrowed from the French; and this criticism was sharpened by the competition between the *Posse* and the imported *comédie-vaudeville*, which is documented in the reviews Nestroy received in 1843 and 1844 (reprinted in the critical apparatus to *HKA: Stücke 19-21*). The debate also underlay the sharpness with which *Das Gewürzkrämer-Kleeblatt* was criticized in 1845 as an aberration, alien to local tradition and a betrayal of Nestroy's true individuality (Schindler 1845: 102).

In the following year Nestroy delighted the critics: *Der Unbedeutende* answered their criteria and in particular presented an unmistakable "moral"; it was indeed the only one of Nestroy's plays that Friedrich Kaiser himself praised as having an improving effect on the self-perception of the "Volk" (Kaiser 1870: 27). With hindsight it is clear that Nestroy was indeed responding to the changed social climate of the Vormärz period but that he was not succumbing to the moralistic ideology of the *Volksstück* (see Boege 1968: 351; Brill 1967: 174), so that the critics who assessed *Der Unbedeutende* in those terms were indulging in wishful thinking. It is revealing that a detached observer such as the young Robert Hamerling (1830-89), attending a performance in 1846, was delighted to find a play matching his ideal of the *Posse* (see Hüttner 1982: 56). Nevertheless Nestroy was widely praised for having struck out in a new direction: *Der Unbedeutende* was a play combining comedy and morality ("ein Stück ..., bei dem die *Komik* und die *Moral* schwesterlich Hand in Hand gehen"), wrote Heinrich Adami (1807-95) in the *Theaterzeitung*; it advanced a healthy, humane teaching ("diese gesunde, körnige, humane Tendenz" [Adami 1846]).

The whole issue was fought out again in 1847 in connection with *Der Schützling*, Nestroy's last full-length play before the 1848 revolution, which sparked off a prolonged debate in the press (see Yates 1993b). Underlying this debate was the continuing sense of crisis in the popular theater, whose whole future seemed to be at stake. Eduard Breier (1811-86), himself a minor playwright, voiced the familiar lament that the genuine *Lokalposse*, rooted in local reality, had collapsed long ago; even Nestroy had descended to vulgarity, relying on "jokes and sarcasm" ("Witz und Sarkasmen"), and it was only in *Der Unbedeutende* that an advance could be seen, with Nestroy at last appealing to the "heart": "Nestroy hat eine Richtung, Nestroy hat einen Weg zum Herzen gefunden!" (Breier 1847: 287). K. Arnold complained about the prevalence of trivial satirical comedies consisting of no more than "scenes thrown together without rhyme or reason, with a few old jokes and a few satirical songs supposed to compensate for the threadbareness of the material" ("jene leidigen Machwerke ..., die aus ohne Sinn und Verstand zusammengewürfelten Szenen bestehen, in denen irgend ein paar abgedroschene Späße herumflattern und ein paar Kouplets für die Armseligkeit des Stoffes entschädigen sollen" [Arnold 1847a: 302]); now, just as Raimund had effected one revolution by introducing moral seriousness, so Nestroy in turn had effected a still more important revolution, broaching "the most urgent social questions"; he had convinced himself that the public was supportive, "and if in his next work he emphasises the serious side of the life of the people more boldly, he will become the creator of the very genre of true popular drama that we have long needed":

> Nestroy hat mit seinen beiden Werken "der Unbedeutende" und "der Schützling" eine viel wichtigere Umwälzung bereits thatsächlich bewirkt. Durch die schneidendsten Gegensätze des wirklichen Lebens regt er in uns die gewichtigsten schwersten Fragen der gesellschaftlichen Verhältnisse an. ... Er hat sich aber nun überzeugt, daß das Publikum ihm gern folgt, und wenn er die ernste Seite des Volkslebens in seinem nächsten Werke noch ungescheuter hervorhebt, so wird er der Schöpfer einer neuen lang entbehrten Gattung eines wahren tüchtigen "Volksschauspieles." (Arnold 1847b: 366)

In *Der Schützling*, the comic element was less dominant than in his other recent works; but still Schindler argued that there was not enough of an emotional appeal, lamenting that the public had "been given a string of dazzling ideas but nothing to touch the heart" ("daß Nestroy ganz und gar vergessen hat, die Gemüthssaite zu berühren. Man hat eine Reihe von brillanten Gedanken vernommen, aber das Herz ging dabei leer aus" [Schindler 1847: 179]). Though *Der Schützling* was not universally praised, it was repeatedly compared with *Der Unbedeutende* as evidence of Nestroy's "new direction." Breier saw him as having entered a new creative phase, abandoning the triviality of the *Posse*, and drew a contrast with *Lumpacivagabundus* and *Das Mädl aus der Vorstadt* (Breier 1847: 290-91). In the *Theaterzeitung*, Raudnitz argued that Nestroy's adoption of a clear moral standpoint betokened a new conception of popular drama; the "inner truth" of his depiction of genuinely popular figures achieved the desired aim of the moral *Volksstück* in raising the consciousness of the *Volk* without descending to divisive polemics (Raudnitz 1847).

Gutt too was drawn into reflecting on the state of Viennese popular drama. The *Lokalposse* of ten years earlier, he argued, had been too limited to last long; Nestroy had been moving towards a new "humorous *Volksstück*," of which there had been intimations in *Der Zerrissene*; he had taken a firm step towards it in *Der Unbedeutende* but had still not attained it in *Der Schützling*, which was essentially a protest against social abuses, as Bauernfeld's *Großjährig* was a protest against political abuses (Gutt 1847a). Saphir too took up the comparison with Bauernfeld: both Nestroy and Bauernfeld had descended to modish polemics ("Zeit-Tendenzen"), with *Der Unbedeutende* and *Der Schützling* approaching the genre of *Ein deutscher Krieger* (Saphir 1847b: 1198). The relevance of the play to contemporary social concerns was widely noted: Adami, for example, stressed that the moral bore directly on present-day reality, "die Bedürfnisse und Tendenzen der Gegenwart" (Adami 1847).

The debate about the didactic *Volksstück* was overtaken by events when revolution broke out in March 1848. Nestroy was quick to take advantage of the brief freedom from censorship to deal directly with the events of the moment; but his satire on the revolution, *Freiheit in Krähwinkel*, at once gave rise to fresh controversy, as the critics tried to decide on which side of the political fence he stood. On the one hand he was attacked in *Der Humorist* for having ridiculed the libertarian cause (März 1848); this was also the view taken by Friedrich Kaiser, who saw the play as containing only "a satire of every libertarian aspiration" ("eine Persiflage aller Freiheitsbestrebungen" [Kaiser 1870: 178]). On the other hand it was also praised as an "ultra-liberal" celebration of the revolution (Anon. 1848). As Hinrich Seeba and Peter Pütz have shown, the misunderstanding was inevitable, given that Nestroy's very material was the libertarian rhetoric of the 1840s and given also the even-handedness of his satire (Seeba 1975; Pütz 1977: 185). It is the only case in Nestroy's career when contemporary critics disagreed fundamentally about the *interpretation* of one of his plays. Otherwise, the reviewers might disagree about the *evaluation* of individual works, and they repeatedly discussed their moral content, their genre, and their relation to their sources; but there was a long time to go before subtleties of *interpretation* entered Nestroy criticism.

In the 1850s Nestroy's productivity declined, partly as a consequence of the responsibility he took on as director of the Carltheater after Carl's death in 1854; and the number of reviewing journals in Vienna declined for a time. But the criteria of the 1840s remained in place. When *Kampl*, for example, was praised in 1852 as the very peak of the Viennese *Posse*, the point was not just its wit (and the comic acting of Scholz and Nestroy) but explicitly its expression of "philosophical" truths, its presentation of human values, its understanding of the human "heart" (X. Rdl. 1852). When Nestroy re-emerged from retirement in 1861, it was still *Der Unbedeutende* that August Silberstein held up as one of the best and most significant plays that had emerged from the popular stage of any nation, "eines der trefflichsten bedeutungsvollsten Stücke, welche die Volksbühne irgend einer Nation besitzt" — praise coupled with regret that Nestroy had not continued on the same lines (Silberstein 1861). By the same token, the issues (and the prejudices) on which critical debate had centred in the 1840s continue to exercise a decisive influence on the interpretation of Nestroy's plays, both in Vienna and beyond it, for the rest of the nineteenth century.

2: The Image of Cynicism

Outside Vienna, Nestroy's reputation even in his own lifetime was divided. As an actor he was a welcome and much-celebrated guest in cities and towns throughout German-speaking Europe, including Hamburg, Berlin, and Munich as well as Prague. For twenty years at the height of his career, despite the immense workload he carried in Vienna as the principal star actor in Karl Carl's company, he went on tour every summer (see Neuber 1987: 185-97). In serious literary circles, by contrast, his name enjoyed little standing. One of the standard German theatrical reference-books of mid-century, latching on to the recurrent objection that he failed to invent "original" material, states not only that he had no power of invention ("durchaus keine Erfindung"), since his material was all borrowed, but that his treatment of it amounted to a debasement ("ein Herabziehen") of the originals (Herlosssohn/Marggraff 1846: 353).

Nestroy's critical rejection in literary circles outside Austria has been traced back to Karl Gutzkow (1811-78) and the Young Germans in mid-century (see Neuber 1987: 113-15). As early as November 1837 Eduard Beurmann's *Frank-furter Telegraph* printed an essay by Franz von Dingelstedt (1814-81) on Austrian literature, in which Nestroy and Hopp are scathingly referred to as the "evangel-ists" of a new age and Nestroy's plays are attacked as corrupting the taste and the morals of Vienna (Dingelstedt 1837: 171). This image of his work, which became very prevalent, was closely related to the established critical orthodoxies in the Viennese press around 1840. Dingelstedt, for example, clearly draws in some respects on the account of Austrian literature just published by Seidlitz, which attacked *Der böse Geist Lumpacivagabundus* and *Zu ebener Erde und erster Stock* (chosen as the only two plays well known outside Vienna) and summed Nestroy up as "the Napoleon of obscenity" ("der Napoleon der Gemeinheit" [Seidlitz 1837: 1: 185]). These orthodoxies were transmitted beyond Austria in the *Morgenblatt für gebildete Leser*, the influential daily published in Stuttgart by Cotta (see Yates 1992), which carried reports ("Korrespondenz-Nachrichten") from "correspon-dents" in Paris, London, and the large German-speaking cities, including Vienna. In the early forties Dingelstedt himself was a "correspondent" from Vienna, which he first visited in 1841. In the late 1830s and early 1840s reports from Vienna appeared irregularly (in 1841, indeed, there were none at all); but they show the picture of Nestroy and of Viennese theater that was presented in Germany to the "educated reader" of the time. That the dialect theater was in decline was repeatedly rehearsed as a statement of fact, and after Carl's takeover of the Theater in der Leopoldstadt in December 1838, the paper mounted repeated attacks on the triviality and indecency of his repertory, especially by comparison with the Theater in der Josefstadt, where under the management of Franz Pokorny the

̄epertory was dominated from 1842 onwards by the enormous box-office success of F. X. Told's spectacular *Zauberstück* in the Raimund manner, *Der Zauberschleier*. The charges directed against Nestroy in particular were specifically those of bad taste, vulgarity, and obscenity. Reporting on the success of *Die verhängnisvolle Faschingsnacht* in 1839, for example, the correspondent of the *Morgenblatt* admitted the "truthfulness" of its depiction of reality (its "lebenswahre Volksscenen") and even its "humor," but lamented that these qualities were outweighed by lack of taste and that Nestroy's talent was betraying every higher standard — "daß ein solches Talent so von allem Geschmack und von höherer Bildung verlassen ist" (Anon. 1839). Four years later the flop of *Nur Ruhe!* produced a still more sweeping condemnation of his alleged squandering of his talent: his muse had "sunk deep into the morass of obscenity" and he must rescue it before it "suffocated" ("Nestroys Muse ist tief in den Schlamm der Gemeinheit versunken; es ist die höchste Zeit, daß er sie zu retten sucht, ehe sie darin erstickt" [Anon. 1844a]). The success of *Eisenbahnheiraten* was commented on at length in a report that must be seen in the context of the rivalry between the indigenous *Posse* and the imported *comédie-vaudeville*: the play confirmed that Nestroy's influence on Viennese dialect drama was thoroughly harmful. By descending into obscenity and moral corruption ("in die Sumpfregion grasser Gemeinheit und Sittenfäulniß") and by depending on verbal wit and burlesque comic effects of exaggerated improbability, he sacrificed the healthy "humor" of traditional popular drama; in this way he provided an insidious example that was followed and taken even further by his less talented successors in feeble plays, often based on French models, and spiced with indecencies and vulgar satirical songs (Anon. 1844b). Even *Der Zerrissene*, for all its comic verve, was held to be marred by coarseness in the characterization of the central figure, Herr von Lips, "eine trostlose Gemeinheit" which was seen as a repellent feature of Nestroy's work in general (Anon. 1844c).

One of the reasons behind this widespread low esteem seems to have been a general failure to distinguish between the actor and the dramatist — though this does not apply to the *Allgemeines Theater-Lexikon* (Herlosssohn/Marggraff 1846), which explicitly saw the *dramatist* Nestroy as representing the characteristics of contemporary Vienna. Especially in the 1840s, observers would note how much Vienna had changed since the early Biedermeier period. Nostalgia for the past would typically find expression in laments for the lost "innocence" of bygone days, which in respect of the theater were often associated with Raimund. In 1840 Friedrich Theodor Vischer (1807-87) explicitly saw this loss of innocence reflected in the dialect theaters, and specifically in the influence of Nestroy. In Raimund's lifetime the "humor" of the dialect theaters had reflected an innocent mood of harlequinade in the city; the decline of popular comedy "at Nestroy's hands" had, Vischer claims, been clear to him as early as 1840: "Schon 1840 trat mir der Verfall der Volkskomödie unter den Händen Nestroys entgegen" (Vischer 1861: 351). In 1841 Gutzkow's *Telegraph für Deutschland* carried a review of Nestroy's appearances in Hamburg in *Glück, Mißbrauch und Rückkehr* and *Der Talisman*, dismissing the "trivialities" of the former play in particular by contrast with the true "humor" of Raimund (Gutzkow 1841); and when four years after that Gutzkow visited Vienna, his memoir of his impressions included a condemnation of the "blasphemous" Nestroy (Gutzkow 1845: 295), who had undermined the whole moral outlook ("sittliche Grundanschauung der Dinge") of the lower classes by the "ambiguity and self-irony" ("die Zweideutigkeit und die Selbstironisirung") in his plays (Gutzkow 1845: 289). It is another striking example of a critical failure to distinguish between the satirist and his subject: when, for example, Schnoferl in *Das Mädl aus der Vorstadt* speaks of the debilitating effect of expressing discontent in nothing more than a pervasive irony, "eine ruhige Sarkasmus-Languissance, wo man über alles räsoniert und andererseits wieder alles akzeptabel find't" (*SW* 11: 12), it is meant precisely as a satirical dig at the very phenomenon Gutzkow attacks. But Gutzkow's condemnation was influential, and disparagement of Nestroy's corrupting effect by contrast with Raimund lives on also in the recollections of the Silesian dramatist Karl von Holtei, twice parodied by Nestroy (in *Weder Lorbeerbaum noch Bettelstab* and *Die verhängnisvolle Faschingsnacht*): whereas Raimund was elevating, he wrote, Nestroy corrupted ("Wo Herr Nestroy herabzog, da erhob Raimund" [Holtei 1872; see Theobald 1993]).

In part these verdicts are revealing of a change in taste, the development of what in England would be known as a typically "Victorian" morality. This is clear from Vischer's disapproval of Offenbach's *Orpheus in the Underworld*, in which he saw Nestroy act in 1860: he expresses disapproval that so "indecent" a piece with its "French frivolity" should have been performed at all in Vienna, and similarly condemns Nestroy in the role of Sansquartier in his version of Angely's comedy *Sieben Mädchen in Uniform* (now boasting the title *Siebzehn Mädchen in Uniform*), in which, Vischer reports, he delivered a series of obscene barrack-room jokes ("eine Reihe von schmierigen Wachstubenzoten") about John of Arc, no doubt in irreverent allusion to Schiller's *Die Jungfrau von Orleans* (Vischer 1861: 351).

Vischer's sharpest charge against Nestroy is that both by word and by gesture he made an impression of indecency, and specifically of bawdy suggestiveness. Once again it is a criticism that appears to be directed particularly at Nestroy's acting rather than at his writing. Nestroy had a range of tones and movements that was "nauseating" to "right feeling," which wanted neither to see the "brutish side of man in all its nakedness" nor to hear "filthy" expressions of scorn or obscene jokes suggesting that the most sacred values of mankind were built around the "phallus":

> Nun aber dieser Nestroy: Er verfügt über ein Gebiet von Tönen und Bewegungen, wo für ein richtiges Gefühl der Ekel, das Erbrechen beginnt. Wir wollen nicht die tierische Natur des Menschen, wie sie sich just auf dem letzten Schritte zum sinnlichsten Genuß gebärdet, in nackter Blöße vors Auge gerückt sehen, wir wollen es nicht hören, dies kotig gemeine "Eh" und "Oh" des Hohns, wo immer ein edleres Gefühl zu beschmutzen ist, wir wollen sie nicht vernehmen, diese stinkenden Witze, die zu erraten geben, daß das innerste Heiligtum der Menschheit einen Phallus verberge. (Vischer 1861: 351)

A voice of even greater weight was that of Friedrich Hebbel. Hebbel was at first an admirer of Nestroy's work. He saw him performing in *Der Schützling* in

Graz in 1847 and his diary records his admiration of Nestroy's talent and his enjoyment of the play (Hebbel 1847); and though during the 1848 revolution he saw the dialect theaters "with their Nestroy" ("die Wiener Vorstadttheater mit ihrem Nestroy") as a potentially dangerous force (Hebbel 1848: 133), early the following year, expressing his liking for a good *Posse*, he wrote that anyone with an understanding of art would give more for a single one of Nestroy's best jokes than for a million run-of-the-mill iambs by a pseudo-poet (Hebbel 1849). Two months after that, however, *Judith und Holofernes*, Nestroy's devastating parody of Hebbel's prose tragedy *Judith*, was performed in the Carltheater, and while there are anecdotal reports that Hebbel showed Nestroy no animosity and even appreciated the force of the parody (Speidel 1881; Blasel 1912), from that point onwards written evidence of his good opinion dries up completely. There is no real reason to doubt the accuracy of Karl Kraus's description of Hebbel as rejecting Nestroy after Nestroy had demolished his tragedy: "[Hebbel], der Nestroy ablehnt, nachdem Nestroys Witz ihm an die tragische Wurzel gegriffen hat" (Kraus 1912a: 16). When Nestroy appeared at the Kai-Theater in 1862, Hebbel alluded critically to the obscenity of his acting as Sansquartier (Hebbel 1862a: 274-75), and after Nestroy's death he wrote dismissively of his "poisonously immoral" farces ("seine giftig-sittenlosen Possen") (Hebbel 1862b: 299). Well into the twentieth century an anecdote of Richard Wagner's was repeated: Hebbel (so Wagner recounted) had said of Nestroy that he had only to sniff at a rose for it to stink (Wagner 1873: 315-16; see Zeidler 1907: 433-34; Meyer 1921: 122).

Among the essays that appeared in the press immediately after his death, none was more virulently hostile than that of Hebbel's close friend Emil Kuh, who debunked the favorable obituaries that had already appeared and laid especial stress on the "unscrupulous" quality of Nestroy's parody. Kuh's essay reviles Nestroy for having delved into the seamier side of life and having offered not characterization but caricature: his indiscriminate cynicism and the obscene suggestiveness of his acting (seemingly balanced by the reassuring qualities of Scholz) had been tolerated by the censor as a safety-valve for social discontent, but Nestroy was incapable of anything but triviality in intention and subject, so that it was quite inappropriate to measure him against Aristophanes: "Er ... kannte aber große Zwecke ebensowenig, als große Stoffe und wichtige Fragen" (Kuh 1862). Kuh's criticism was quoted in the standard Austrian biographical reference-book of the late nineteenth century, which recorded that Nestroy had depicted abjectly corrupt figures and had exercised a malign influence by introducing a quality of indecency previously unknown in Viennese popular drama (Wurzbach 1869).

Rainer Theobald has recently challenged the assumption that all these negative judgments are simply blinkered, and that the viewpoint of hindsight is necessarily superior. To the extent that the various critics' rejection was based on direct experience of seeing productions in the theater, especially with Nestroy himself acting, we do well, he argues, not to dismiss it out of hand (Theobald 1993). Clearly, however, some of the evidence is anecdotal and second-hand; moreover, the charge of indecency lived on in literary histories, in which Nestroy's acting had no part to play. Late-nineteenth-century literary historians schooled by expectations of "realism" had no sympathy for his satire. This remains true even of accounts generally sympathetic to him, such as that by Otto von Leixner, who fully recognizes the genius of his wit but qualifies this recognition with an allusion to his exaggerations and his weakness for *double entendre* (Leixner 1906: 920-21). That Nestroy is recurrently contrasted with Raimund in the literary histories reflects a habit of thinking established among journalistic reviewers in his own lifetime. What is striking is that (again, even in accounts that place a high value on his work) the contrast is often stated exclusively in terms of a deficiency in Nestroy: thus even Leixner, treating his abandoning of the *Zauberstück* in the mid-1830s in favor of the *Lokalposse*, describes him not only as being of a different (less "naive") mentality but as specifically *lacking* Raimund's "poetic gifts":

> Er versuchte es zuerst, sich zwischen Meisl und Raimund zu halten, und schrieb noch Zauberstücke ("Nagerl und Handschuh"). Aber bald wandte er sich von dieser Gattung ab, für die ihm die poetische Begabung und die Naivität fehlten, um sich ganz der derben Lokalposse zuzuwenden. (Leixner 1906: 920-21)

The sense that Nestroy's work (and acting — the two often not distinguished) had a specifically destructive power is reflected in the responsibility ascribed to him for both social and political change. Laube's memoirs, for example, written in the 1870s, blame his influence for a damaging tendency in Vienna to indulge in negative carping — an inevitable consequence, as he puts it, when the popular clown is a Mephisto: "Das ist unvermeidlich, wenn der Schalksnarr der Vorstadt Mephisto heißt" (Laube 1875-80: 203-4). Also in the 1870s a major two-volume history of the 1848 revolution appeared in which Nestroy's plays, with their attention to social reality and their mocking tone, are credited with having stimulated in the pleasure-loving audiences a new critical spirit fundamental to the development of a revolutionary atmosphere (Reschauer 1872: 16-18). Again that is meant critically; such commentators were essentially rejecting as subversive a radicalism in Nestroy that later critics (especially but by no means exclusively those of Marxist outlook) would seize on as one of their main lines of interpretation.

Moritz Necker rightly records that adverse judgments such as those of Laube and Kuh accurately reflect literary opinion in their time (Necker 1891: 207-8). It frequently happens, of course, that an author's reputation sinks in the years following his or her death; but in Nestroy's case the problem was exacerbated by the fact that he was remembered so vividly as an actor. Bauernfeld voiced what seems to have been a widespread belief that it was impossible to perform the plays without Nestroy himself to act in them: "Man kann Nestroy nicht ohne Nestroy spielen" (Bauernfeld 1873: 59). In fact, after his death, his work was still frequently performed in Vienna (see Hüttner 1964, 1975), and in 1881, to celebrate the centenary of the old Theater in der Leopoldstadt, the Carltheater under the direction of Franz Tewele launched a Nestroy cycle, which was originally planned as a "Nestroy week" but which proved so successful that it was extended into a Nestroy festival lasting seven weeks and presenting no fewer than twenty plays (Hüttner 1964: 2: 46-47). Ludwig Speidel, one of the most perceptive critics at that time, published a brief memoir celebrating the combination of wit and moral indignation that underlay Nestroy's apparent cynicism; the power of his satirical scorn was, Speidel argues, capable at times of rising to Swiftian heights (Speidel 1881: 2). Friedrich Schlögl (1821-92), a popular Viennese journalist who claimed that his memory went back to the première of *Lumpacivagabundus* (though he had been only twelve at the time) published a defence of Nestroy against the charge of debasing popular comic tradition. Schlögl pointed to works like *Der Zerrissene, Kampl, Der Schützling*, and above all *Der Unbedeutende*, and posed the rhetorical question whether even Raimund could have drawn the character of Peter Span with more human warmth (Schlögl 1883: 147). Had those who belittled Nestroy, he asked, not read these works?

It was a pertinent question. The works he lists *had* been published; but most of the plays had not, so that critical judgments depended largely on impressions (or memories) of stage performances. This is a consequence of the lack of copyright protection in the mid-nineteenth century. By contract, a play was the property of the theater company while it was in manuscript, and as soon it was available for general sale in print it could be performed anywhere without fee. As a result, printed texts were often slow to appear. In Nestroy's case only seventeen of his plays were printed in his lifetime (most of those published by the Viennese firm of Wallishausser, which specialized in the theater). Memorable *bons mots* from his plays had become proverbial even in his lifetime (see Silberstein 1861), and after his death pithy quotations were anthologized, notably in Rosner's collection of 1873, which was reprinted several times and contributed to fixing the popular image of Nestroy in the period (see Obermaier 1988a: 120); but critics had to derive their impressions of whole plays mainly from theatrical productions until the first collected edition appeared, nearly thirty years after his death, in 1890-91.

That edition would include the first printed texts of two plays containing passages that have dogged Nestroy criticism. One is from the early parody *Weder Lorbeerbaum noch Bettelstab*, in which the bibulous harpist Leicht, a beer-house entertainer and would-be playwright, disclaims all higher artistic aspirations. He does not aspire to the laurel wreath, he claims; his plays are meant to be entertaining, to make the public laugh and to earn money for himself. To write comedies and aspire to a laurel wreath would be a "mixture of stupidity and arrogance," much as if a humble pastry-cook were to give himself airs by pretending his Christmas sweetmeats made him a rival of the sculptor Canova:

> Bis zum Lorbeer versteig' ich mich nicht. G'fallen sollen meine Sachen, unter-
> halten, lachen sollen d'Leut', und mir soll d'G'schicht' a Geld tragen, daß ich
> auch lach', das is der ganze Zweck. G'spaßige Sachen schreiben und damit nach
> dem Lorbeer trachten wollen, das is eine Mischung von Dummheit und Arro-
> ganz, das is grad so, als wie wenn einer Zwetschgenkrampus macht und gibt sich
> für einen Rivalen von Canova aus. (*SW* 3: 355-56)

The second is from a play dating from the mid-1830s, *Die beiden Nachtwand-ler*, and is again spoken by the figure played by Nestroy himself, in this case the cynical Fabian Strick, who observes that he always believes the worst of everyone and has "seldom been disappointed":

Ich glaube von jedem Menschen das Schlechteste, selbst von mir, und ich hab'
mich noch selten getäuscht. (*SW* 6: 311)

The first passage was often assumed, even by Nestroy's supporters and
admirers (e.g. Silberstein 1861; Rosner 1910: 173; Berger 1912), to be a statement
of his own modesty; in fact it is at most self-irony, a *satirical* summary of an attitude
associated with the dramatists of the popular theater, spiced with an element of
commercial calculation which is geared to Nestroy's specifically parodistic purpose. The second is a statement of universal scepticism about human motivation
which in its dramatic context — it is directed at the rope-maker Sebastian Faden
— is actually proved to be quite unfounded. That is, both statements belong in a
particular dramatic context; there is nothing in either to stamp them as being in
any way confessional statements of an authorial credo. Neither even comes in one
of the long satirical monologues which work as breaks in the fictional plot and in
which the central figures (most of them acted by Nestroy himself) reflect generally
on life.

To identify the dramatist with his characters, or the actor-dramatist with
the roles he played, is critically naive; but the image has proved an extremely
tenacious one. Nestroy was stamped as a cynic and the purveyor of trivial comedy
not to be taken seriously, and the two quotations, wrenched out of context, have
been made to do yeoman service over and over again.

Both, for example, are quoted, ascribed to Nestroy himself as statements of
his principles, in the entry on Nestroy in the standard German biographical
reference-work, the *Allgemeine deutsche Biographie*. The article is a good example
of the orthodox perception of Nestroy before the appearance of the first collected
edition. The author, the Hebbel scholar Richard Maria Werner, sees Nestroy's
drama as growing out of imitation of Raimund, with a parodistic element from
the start, and defines this parodistic element as a consistent feature of the whole
of his *oeuvre*: "Parodie ist das Losungswort, welches uns aus allen Stücken
Nestroy's entgegen tönt" (Werner 1886: 449). On this basis Werner compares
Nestroy's work with Raimund's, to Nestroy's disadvantage: everything is presented
in coarser, unidealizing terms ("Alles ist ins Gemeine gezogen"), the "genuine
poetry" which was Raimund's achievement is ridiculed, debased, and finally
destroyed (450). His "diabolical" character emerged fully in the forties under
French influence, as he mocked even the most sublime qualities and sought out
the very worst in human nature. Werner's view of Nestroy here is close to Kuh's:
everything was grist to the mill of Nestroy's "cynicism," and he could, indeed, be
regarded as the very personification of the destructive spirit that underlay the
revolution of 1848 (451). Werner concedes the inventiveness and abundance of
Nestroy's wit, and lays weight both on the skill of his parodistic medleys (*Quod-
libets*) and on his successful literary parody of Hebbel in *Judith und Holofernes*
(454); but this leads him back to contrasting Nestroy's "parodistic comedy"
(mocking, clever, negative) with Raimund's "humor" (sentimental, naive, idealizing), and he sums them up as polar opposites, Raimund an "idealist," Nestroy a
"pessimist":

Raimund's Humor war rührende Kindlichkeit, welche mit weit offenen Augen in die Welt starrte, Nestroy's bizarre Laune war superkluge Gescheitheit, welche die Mängel der Welt mit scharfen Augen erfaßte; Raimund scheint immer wie aus einem schönen Traume, der noch in ihm nachzittert, zur traurigen Wirklichkeit zu erwachen, Nestroy dagegen alles Schöne, Edle auf Erden für einen phantastischen Traum und nur den Schmutz für Wirklichkeit zu halten; jeder ist Idealist, dieser Pessimist .... (454)

Werner also argues that it was mistaken to base a judgment of Nestroy's works on the few printed texts then available, because of the discrepancy between the printed text and the version that one was likely to see performed in the theater, which would contain additions passed down from Nestroy's own time (452). Divergencies between the first printed versions and theater manuscripts (and indeed Nestroy's autograph manuscripts) are indeed common, and it is only in the new critical edition (*HKA*) that they are being documented as fully as possible. However, the first important step in making Nestroy's works available in print — a first step, then, to creating any kind of a basis for objective scholarly study — was taken in 1890-91 with the appearance of the first collected edition, edited by two journalists and minor playwrights, Vincenz Chiavacci (1847-1916) and Ludwig Ganghofer (1855-1920).

Timed to appear before the copyright on Nestroy's work ran out (the period of protection was then only thirty years after an author's death), this edition contained texts of sixty-three plays, based on theater manuscripts. Only two of the plays that had been printed in Nestroy's lifetime were missing, *Theaterg'schichten durch Liebe, Intrige, Geld und Dummheit* and the parody *Tannhäuser*, in all forty-eight were published for the first time, including one important work unperformed in Nestroy's lifetime and so made known for the first time. This was *Der alte Mann mit der jungen Frau*, described as a fragment and given the generic designation "Volksstück mit Gesang in vier Akten" (*CG* 11: 115), which is not corroborated by any surviving manuscript. A whole number of other texts which are now established among Nestroy's best-known plays were made available in print for the first time; these included *Das Haus der Temperamente, Die beiden Nachtwandler, Liebesgeschichten und Heiratssachen, Der Schützling, Lady und Schneider, Judith und Holofernes, Höllenangst*, and the late one-act play *Frühere Verhältnisse*. The list speaks for itself; only now could readers begin to form a rounded impression of Nestroy's work.

The edition was produced at great speed. Work on it began only in mid-1889, when the editors applied to Nestroy's daughter-in-law Stephanie Nestroy-Bene for permission to edit his plays from the manuscripts in her possession and duly received a crate of material for that purpose (see Gladt 1967: 11-12). The editors' preface describes their working methods. Though they based their text on theater manuscripts (copies rather than autograph originals), they defined their editorial task very liberally: it included choosing between possible variants, selecting the one they thought most effective theatrically and closest to what they adjudged the authentic Nestroy spirit; rephrasing stage directions in the interest of editorial consistency; and imposing uniformity in the reproduction of dialect forms (*CG* 1: viii). The printed text, then, reflects a considerable degree of editorial intervention. From a letter written by Chiavacci it seems, moreover, that the manuscripts were used not just as the source of the text but physically as the basis of the edition, being cut up for that purpose (see Gladt 1967: 13) and no doubt destroyed afterwards: none of the manuscripts on which the edition is based appear to have survived, and certainly by 1898 Chiavacci claimed to have none of them in his possession any more (see Gladt 1967: 13). It may even be that some autograph manuscripts were lost in this way; although Nestroy carefully preserved his manuscripts, including many rough notes and drafts, there are now significant gaps in the extant fair copies, notably those of plays dating from the years 1837-38 and 1845-46. The survival of his autograph manuscripts after his death was, however, so chancy (see Chapter 3 below) that they may have been lost in other ways.

Despite the unsatisfactory editorial procedures adopted by Chiavacci and Ganghofer, their edition is extremely important, and not just for the impact it made in its time. For the text of some plays, which were not printed in Nestroy's lifetime and for which no manuscripts of any kind survive, it is the sole source. These include the text of *Eine Wohnung ist zu vermieten*, now regarded as a work central to the canon. The version of *Die beiden Herrn Söhne* that was actually performed in 1845 is preserved partly in a fragmentary manuscript which contains most of the first two acts; the rest of this version survives only in the text published by Chiavacci and Ganghofer. In the case of *Kampl*, the text in *CG* is based on a manuscript independent of the first printed edition; because it is closer than any other source to Nestroy's draft (which survives in an autograph manuscript) it helps to authenticate the draft as the basis of the eventual fair copy, now lost (see *HKA: Stücke 31*: 493).

In its final volume the edition includes the first large-scale Nestroy monograph, written by another journalist, Moritz Necker (1857-1915). This gives a chronological account of Nestroy's career, filled out with quotations from the Viennese press and from a well-chosen selection of relevant memoirs. It is a popularizing essay, as the situation demanded, but it also contains some useful pointers, as in an extended comparison of *Der böse Geist Lumpacivagabundus* with Nestroy's source, Carl Weisflog's story "Das große Los" (Necker 1891: 133-36), and some astute perceptions. Necker is, for example, sensible of the specifically *comic* excellence of *Glück, Mißbrauch und Rückkehr*, and in considering its treatment of the contrast between city and country, he stresses Nestroy's avoidance of Raimund-like "sentimentality" (158-59). He consistently fails, however, to do justice to the complexity of Nestroy's work. A play such as *Einen Jux will er sich machen*, for instance, which reflects satirically the oppressive social stagnation and the materialism of the late Biedermeier period (see Preisner 1968: 96-97; May 1975: 171-76; Ahrens 1982: 235-44; Hein 1983b) is taken by Necker as a work of "pure gaiety," and nothing more (168-69). He presents Nestroy as having had a "pessimistic" view of human nature and as tending to "realism" in his writing (140); and he also oversimplifies Nestroy's ideological position in the pre-revolutionary plays, reducing *Der Unbedeutende* to the expression of a "democratic" idea (180) and seeing *Der Schützling* as evidence of his keeping pace with the liberalism of his times: "Nestroy schreitet, wie man sieht, mit seiner Zeit mit, er ist ein

Liberaler in jeder Beziehung" (181). In *Freiheit in Krähwinkel* again Necker sees only the spirit of the revolution and criticism of restrictions in the Metternich period (184). He also extols *Kampl* as an edifying "Volksstück" (189), an evaluation typical of the period: it is revealing, for example, that the comic actor Karl Blasel (1831-1922), who thought it Nestroy's greatest work, would later proudly recall the verdict of Louis Grois, one of the leading members of Carl's company, that his performance of the title role was more "sentimental" than Nestroy's had been (Blasel 1912).

Though Necker stresses the importance of Nestroy the dramatist, as opposed to the actor (208-9), he still approaches the plays as having been basically vehicles for Carl's (and later Nestroy's) company; that is, he assumes that Nestroy's priority lay in creating theatrical roles rather than in constructing works of art centring on well-designed plots (216). So too his view of the set pieces, the monologues and satirical songs written for Nestroy's own acting, is that by his later years they had degenerated into a mere theatrical routine (217).

Into the early years of the twentieth century, there was little challenge to the perspectives established by Werner and Necker. When Hans Sittenberger (1863-1943), a well-known writer on contemporary drama, attempted a reassessment, it consisted largely of a chronological account, based on Necker; Nestroy is presented as an heir of Hanswurst, in his weaknesses as in his strengths (Sittenberger 1901: 148). Sittenberger, who takes no account of the unsatisfactory evidential authority of the 1890-91 text, shows next to no understanding of the subtleties of Nestroy's language. He rightly recognizes the dominant influence it would exercise on Anzengruber (126) but belittles its quality because of its frequent "incorrectness" by the standards of formal written German, concluding from Nestroy's offences against the rules of grammar that he lacked understanding of the true value of education (127). Sittenberger has a similarly unsympathetic approach to Nestroy's characterization, which, applying the orthodox criteria of realist drama, he finds impoverished; the conclusion he draws is that Nestroy lacked the capacity to create a unified character (144). He takes over all the conventional assumptions about Nestroy's methods of writing: if, like Bauernfeld, he alluded to contemporary events, these allusions are, Sittenberger asserts, irrelevant to the action of the play, and are not carefully embedded in it; indeed, a dependence on extemporization is in his view the key to Nestroy's artistic individuality (141-42). His most perceptive points are indebted to Werner: he stresses the parodistic force of Nestroy's comic acting (143) and extends the point to his writing, describing him as having been so essentially a parodist that even works which were not written as parodies look as though they were; parody is "die ihm eigenthümliche Form, sich zu geben" (160-61). Sittenberger rightly draws attention to a detectable growth in the political interest evidenced in Nestroy's work but follows Necker in his diagnosis of his political sympathies, describing him as subscribing to the liberal demands of the revolution (164).

Sittenberger's approach is hampered by his adoption of fundamentally anachronistic criteria, as is given away by an allusion to the "titanic" Anzengruber (126). Four years later Stefan Hock (1877-1947), a dramaturg at the Burgtheater, would indeed treat Nestroy essentially as a milestone in the development of Viennese popular drama towards Anzengruber (Hock 1905). So too Alfred von Berger (1853-1912), a prominent critic and man of the theater who was director of the Burgtheater from 1910 to 1912, would summarize Nestroy's achievement as having lain in making popular drama "realistic and modern," and would argue that this was the very centre of his whole work: "Nestroy hat das Volksstück realistisch und modern gemacht, das war, knapp gefaßt, der Kern seines Lebenswerkes" (Berger 1912). Hock once again contrasts Nestroy with Raimund, to Raimund's advantage; he traces the increasing politicization of dialect comedy, comparing Nestroy with Friedrich Kaiser in this respect, with the *Posse* being transformed in 1848 into a dramatization of contemporary events (43); he suggests (very unconvincingly) that the influence of Balzac is reflected in Nestroy's more realistic presentation of craftsmen by comparison with Bäuerle (41), and accepts the conventional contemporary condemnation of his malign influence on the Viennese public (42). Like Werner and Sittenberger, he sees parody as Nestroy's true province (37); but the plays he singles out for praise are the more edifying and arguably more didactic works of 1846-47, *Der Unbedeutende* and *Der Schützling* (in which he sees Nestroy writing a "social *Volksstück*" [42]), and above all *Kampl*, which he sees as Nestroy's "masterpiece," his "most perfect *Volksstück*" (45).

Such, then, was the orthodox view around the turn of the century of Nestroy's historical place in the development of popular drama. That this image remained largely negative in the first decade or so of the twentieth century is shown, for example, in essays by two prominent literary historians, Jakob Zeidler (1855-1911) and Wilhelm Kosch (1879-1960). Zeidler, defining Nestroy's world-view as one of resignation and pessimism, contrasts it with that of Raimund, maintaining that what Nestroy provides is a satiric and parodistic distortion of the real world (Zeidler 1907). Kosch's article presents Nestroy solely in the context of the growth of realism in Viennese dialect comedy from the early nineteenth century onwards and sees his career in terms of a development away from Raimund and the *Zauberstück* genre, with *Zu ebener Erde und erster Stock*, a part-serious, part-comic social "Volksstück," marking the decisive break (Kosch 1912: 22).

Stirrings of dissent from this kind of orthodoxy were rare. One notable exception is a review by Hermann Bahr (1863-1934), the most vocal apostle of Modernism in Vienna, of a production of *Der Zerrissene* in the Raimundtheater in 1896. Bahr's starting-point is Nestroy's continued proven effectiveness in performance, and in this Bahr compares him positively with the datedness of Raimund. Nestroy, he argues, belonged to a new age; his unsparing rationality perceived the comic contrast between the new age and older conventions:

> Deutlicher müßte man sagen, daß er ein ganz neuer Mensch gewesen ist, der nichts von der Vergangenheit in sich hatte. ... Ganz neue Wesen sieht er sich noch in ganz alten Formen bewegen; das kommt ihm komisch vor. (Bahr 1899: 463)

Bahr too compares Nestroy to Balzac — not, however, in relation to supposedly realistic characterization, as Sittenberger would do, but in his awareness of fundamental change: "durch alle Nebel hat er schon die Linien der neuen Zeit erblickt" (464). The stress on the "new" is typical of Bahr, and in his approach to Nestroy it is a strength, in that it enables him to shake free of the clichés of the literary historians and to argue the undiminished relevance of Nestroy's work to the modern world. *Der Zerrissene* was, he claimed, just one example of this characteristic modernity: Lips was an utterly modern figure, so that the play might stand as a satire on the coffee-house decadents of the *fin de siècle* (464-66). In claiming Nestroy for the modern movement, Bahr was ahead of his times; it was not until 1912 that a more comprehensive revaluation got under way.

3: The Nestroy Renaissance

The prejudices that had blackened Nestroy's image in the second half of the nineteenth century proved tenacious. They are enshrined in a number of standard German reference books on the history of literature or of drama. One example is a two-volume survey of German literature, first published in 1916, by Richard M. Meyer (1860-1914), who had held a chair in Berlin. Meyer's account follows the lines established by Kuh and Werner (Kuh 1862; Werner 1886). Nestroy appears in his familiar role as the diametrical opposite of Raimund, debasing both the *Posse* and its performance by an "innate" cynicism: "Sein Zynismus entspringt weder der Notwehr noch dem Übermut, sondern einfach angeborner Gemeinheit" (Meyer 1921: 122). Meyer ascribes to Nestroy himself Fabian Strick's line in *Die beiden Nachtwandler* about believing the worst of everyone, quotes the adverse judgments of Vischer and Hebbel, and presents Nestroy as rejecting everything elevated — hence his excellence as a parodist, in that (according to Meyer) he regarded everything poetic and all idealism as illusory: "Er hält im Grunde alle Poesie und allen Idealismus wirklich für Schwindel" (122). The approach adopted by Meyer, and by Werner before him, was later summed up Leopold Liegler: some people, he observed, are thrown by the very freedom of thought which is fundamental to Nestroy's way of writing (Liegler 1930: 10).

Another example is the history of German comedy by Theodor Holl, professor of literary history in Karlsruhe. Here again the sarcastic Nestroy is contrasted with the idealist Raimund: by contrast with the moral content of Raimund's work, Nestroy provided a "naturalistic portrait of corruption" ("an Stelle sittlicher Forderung naturalistisches Abbild des Verkommenen"), anticipating the naturalism of the early twentieth century by the presentation of social contrasts in *Zu ebener Erde und erster Stock*. Holl concedes Nestroy's parodistic wit and his attainment of grotesque effects, but judges him lacking in deeper "humor" founded in experience, and consequently failing to transcend his material (Holl 1923: 251-52).

These extraordinary misjudgments were already very dated by the 1920s. A major revival of interest in Nestroy had got under way in 1912, stimulated by the fiftieth anniversary of his death, and prompting a reassessment of his critical reputation. There were by then a number of one-volume editions of selected plays on the market, notably those by Otto Rommel (1908) and Fritz Brukner (1911). Fritz Brukner (1881-1944) was a collector, whose private collection of manuscripts and other material eventually passed into the hands of the Stadt- und Landesbibliothek in Vienna. Otto Rommel (1880-1965), a Viennese schoolmaster who devoted himself for half a century to the study of Viennese dialect theater, is one of two figures with whom the revival in Nestroy's reputation is principally associated. The other is the great Viennese satirist Karl Kraus (1874-1936), who recognized in Nestroy a forerunner of his own linguistic satire. The revival developed, then, along two complementary tracks: Rommel treated Nestroy essentially within the framework of a local Viennese tradition of "popular" (that is, dialect) comedy stretching back to the Baroque theater and forward to the realism of Anzengruber; Kraus presented him essentially as a master of satirical language.

The fiftieth anniversary of Nestroy's death fell at a time when literature, theater, indeed all the arts were standing at a crossroads, reflecting the changed perceptions and rapidly changing social structures of the age. It was a highly propitious time for revaluation. Max Reinhardt (1873-1943), the most celebrated Austrian theatrical producer of the *avant garde*, had been mounting Nestroy productions in Berlin since 1904, and had added *Der böse Geist Lumpacivagabundus* for the first time in 1910. But Nestroy's most forceful champion was one of Reinhardt's most outspoken critics, Karl Kraus. Kraus read his celebratory paper "Nestroy und die Nachwelt" to an audience of over a thousand in the great hall of the Musikverein building in Vienna on 2 May, and it appeared in print in his journal *Die Fackel* eleven days later (Kraus 1912a).

"Nestroy und die Nachwelt" is essentially an essay about satire; at the end Kraus draws the threads of his evidence together in a final definition of satire as an art in tension with its time, at once its "product" and its "despairing opposite," "ihr Produkt und ihr hoffnungsloses Gegenteil" (23). The formulation suggests the extent to which Kraus saw in Nestroy a precursor of his own work, a prophet of the apocalyptic decline he observed in the Austria of his own times; and his shafts are partly directed against his own recurrent targets, including both Reinhardt and Hugo von Hofmannsthal. But the perspective of hindsight, the context of "posterity," also provides a starting-point for an extended celebration of Nestroy, rectifying the critical rejection that his reputation had suffered in the later nineteenth century. His artistry was unrecognized by posterity, Kraus argues, because the "dynamite" of his satire is concealed in the protective wrapping of a conventional comic formula: "weil er sein Dynamit in Watte wickelte" (5). What his use of borrowed plots reveals is not derivativeness but his creativeness, the originality and imaginative power of his language being such that he can conjure up a personality in a few words, a whole setting in a sentence as no other German comic dramatist could (7) — a point later illustrated by Kraus in the essay "Die Wortgestalt" with an example from *Die verhängnisvolle Faschingsnacht* (Kraus 1921: 73). Nestroy's satire is "sprachverbuhlt" (Kraus 1912a: 7), rooted in a fascinated love of language and with a Shakespearian vividness (10); he is "the first German satirist in whom language itself reflects on the things it expresses" ("der erste deutsche Satiriker, in dem sich die Sprache Gedanken macht über die Dinge" [12]). His use of dialect (in contrast to Anzengruber's) serves a genuine artistic function: "Nestroys Dialekt ist Kunstmittel, nicht Krücke" (15). That is, as Hans Weigel would spell out over half a century later, Nestroy's language is not an authentic reflection of dialect; indeed, dialect forms only a part of the linguistic registers in which he achieves his effects (Weigel 1972: 92).

Kraus's determination not to let Nestroy be devalued as a mere purveyor of local color led to his criticism of Leopold Liegler (Kraus 1925: 25-28), who published an edition of *Eine Wohnung ist zu vermieten*, attempting to transcribe the text in a spelling closer to spoken Viennese than Nestroy's own (Liegler 1925a) — the first volume of a planned edition of twenty plays, the typescripts for eighteen of which are preserved in the *Brenner* Archive in the University of Innsbruck (see Stieg 1991). Kraus firmly restated his position, quoting his insistence in "Nestroy und die Nachwelt" on Nestroy's stature as a "German satirist."

Kraus's sense of his own deep affinity to Nestroy is also manifested in his definition of Nestroy's work as a sustained creation of a role, "written acting" ("geschriebene Schauspielkunst" [Kraus 1912a: 8]), and also in his resistance towards any reduction of Nestroy's satire to a fixed political outlook. In 1908, rejecting a politically-motivated reading of *Freiheit in Krähwinkel* as a work supporting the Liberal cause, he had insisted that its satirical thrust was directed not so much against the forces of right-wing reaction as against the revolution itself (Kraus 1908: 1) — so going considerably further than Hock's recognition of a double-edged quality in the satire (Hock 1905: 43). In particular he attacked Necker's biography for reducing Nestroy to a bland respectable liberalism (Kraus 1912b: 29-30). Later he would wonder whether he might not have gone too far in his attempts to defend Nestroy against getting appropriated by the liberal camp ("in dem Bestreben, Nestroy gegen liberale Berufungen zu schützen" [Kraus 1923: 52]); but the central point at issue, which is stated most fully in "Nestroy und die Nachwelt," is his conviction that the true satiric artist is bound to be "verwirrend gesinnungslos," uncommitted to any ideological allegiance (Kraus 1912a: 17). In this he would be followed both by Liegler and by Egon Friedell (Liegler 1930; Friedell 1932). Underlining the honesty of Nestroy's satire, Liegler writes of his impartiality towards all ideology; the strength of his satire derived from a "lack of character" (that is, an avoidance of subjective slanting) that afforded a true inner freedom, committed only to human values and not to slogans, "seeing the world whole and with a steady gaze":

> jene beneidenswerte Charakterlosigkeit, welche die wahre innere Freiheit ver-
> bürgt, welche sich nur dem menschlichen Wert, nie aber den Phrasen und
> Schlagworten verpflichtet fühlt. Aus solcher Charakterlosigkeit fließt die Kraft
> und die menschliche Berechtigung der Nestroyschen Satire. Nur wer hellen
> Blicks wie er in die Welt sieht und vor nichts das Auge schließt, kann sie
> bewältigen .... (Liegler 1930: 18-19)

Kraus's argument is that Nestroy's satire is not polemical but essentially creative — "nie polemisch, immer schöpferisch" (Kraus 1912a: 10) — and that its range is comprehensive, in respect of society, politics, and culture: "Er stieß oben an die Bildung an und unten an die Banalität" (16). The result is a form of satire in advance of its age: "Was hat Nestroy gegen seine Zeitgenossen? Wahrlich, er übereilt sich. Er geht antizipierend seine kleine Umwelt mit einer Schärfe an, die einer späteren Sache würdig wäre" (20-21). In view of his constant ridiculing of Bahr, it would have been galling for Kraus to know that Bahr had beaten him to this last point by many years, in his 1896 review of *Der Zerrissene*: "Oft ist seine Satire ihren Gegenständen vorgegangen" (Bahr 1899: 464). Berger too had a similar point to make in 1912 in relation to the political scene in particular: many a prominent Viennese figure of the last twenty-five years, he observed, gave the impression of being a product of Nestroy's inspired invention and had been cheated of immortality only because Nestroy was already long dead (Berger 1912).

Kraus retained a lifelong admiration of Nestroy, repeatedly restating, in varying formulations, his conviction that he was the greatest satirical thinker in the German language, "der im Sprachwitz tiefste, bis zur Lyrik unerbittlichste satirische Denker Deutschlands" (Kraus 1922c: 71). He would complain about the phalanx of conventional *idées fixes* both in the theater and in the press (e.g. Kraus 1912b, 1922b: 53), and in effect fought a campaign to establish Nestroy as a classic (see Rössler 1981: 28), especially by comparison with more academically respectable contemporaries such as the recognized Austrian classic, Grillparzer, for whom Kraus had a blind spot; he declared that in every line he wrote Nestroy was more of a poet, a dramatist, an epigrammatist than Grillparzer was in his whole *oeuvre* (Kraus 1922a: 13). He gave readings of Nestroy from 1912 onwards, most frequently in the period 1922-26 as part of the one-man "Theater der Dichtung" with which he attempted to re-establish the primacy of the spoken word in drama, by contrast with the stage effects indulged in by Reinhardt and the liberties taken in the Burgtheater; his polemic against the Burgtheater culminated in his essay "Nestroy und das Burgtheater," written as a defence of Nestroy against the damage inflicted on him in a new production of *Lumpaci-vagabundus* (Kraus 1925). A further spin-off from his readings was that he also published his own adaptations of two plays, *Die beiden Nachtwandler* (1920) and *Der konfuse Zauberer* (1925).

The success of Kraus's many-pronged public campaign for the recognition of Nestroy's stature can be seen in the judgments of critics influenced by him such as Liegler, who regarded *Einen Jux will er sich machen* in particular as evidence that Nestroy was a theatrical genius of the first magnitude ("ein Bühnengenie erster Größe"), or Otto Stoessl (1875-1936), who presented Nestroy as the one really great writer of comedies not just in Austria but in the German language (Liegler 1930: 11; Stoessl 1935: 218).

While Kraus campaigned on Nestroy's behalf in his essay and readings, academic research was steadily continuing in the field of theater history and history of drama. Moriz Enzinger's two-volume study of thematic continuities in the theatrical tradition of Viennese popular comedy, stretching back to Baroque roots, places Nestroy within this framework (Enzinger 1918-19). Enzinger traces his use of material drawn from contemporary life back to the "Sittenstück" of the late eighteenth and the beginning of the nineteenth century (15); he sees his consistently "parodistic" use of the allegorical framework of the *Zauberstück* as having been anticipated in Raimund (47) and his comic figures as being descended from Hanswurst. Enzinger also modifies the line taken by Sittenberger, who had read the early romantic drama *Prinz Friedrich* simply as an ambitious failure (Sittenberger 1901: 162), arguing that it reads like an unintentional parody of the pathos of the early-eighteenth-century *Haupt- und Staatsaktionen* (456). He stresses that Nestroy enlarges the scope of parody in the dialect theater, creating a new form of "satiric parody," and describes *Judith und Holofernes* as his parodistic masterpiece (467-68). Both Kraus and Friedell would also place particular emphasis on the parodistic force of this work in its exposure of the hollowness of the Hebbel tragedy (Kraus 1917; Friedell 1932: 282). Enzinger identifies parodistic technique as a fundamental part of Nestroy's work, and sees it reflected also in the "bitterness" of *Der Unbedeutende, Der alte Mann mit der jungen Frau*, and the "cynical" *Kampl* (468); he argues that in Nestroy the devices of parody are applied to satire, so that Nestroy produces what he calls "eine Parodie des Lebens" (471). The unclarity of the term, which blurs the fundamental aesthetic distinction between parody and satire, exposes the unsureness of Enzinger's interpretative judgment.

Knowledge about the theatrical background to Nestroy's work was also advanced by Kraus's publication of Gutt's accounts of his performances in Prague in 1844 (Kraus 1924). The excerpts are accurately transcribed, and though they are not all complete, and are drawn from only the one season, they were seized on as providing a more solid basis for subsequent discussion of Nestroy's acting than most of the reviews in the *Theaterzeitung* and other Viennese papers (see Rommel 1930: 185). In the meantime there had been a steady stream of other discoveries. R. F. Arnold identified the source of *Einen Jux will er sich machen*, a one-act English comedy by John Oxenford, *A Day Well Spent* (Arnold 1923); and no fewer than four more plays, which were thought to have been lost, were rediscovered. Brukner published texts of *Der Zettelträger Papp* and *Moppels Abenteuer* in 1910, both edited from theater manuscripts; Karl Glossy published *Häuptling Abendwind* in the *Neue Freie Presse* in 1912, thereby drawing from Karl Kraus, who at once perceived the satirical force of the play, a rare expression of gratitude to the *Neue Freie Presse* (Kraus 1912b: 33); and in 1921 Peter Sturmbusch published an edition of *"Nur keck!"*, of which a nearly complete autograph manuscript had survived.

The exact nature of the material destroyed in 1890-91 during the production of the first collected edition (*CG*) can only be speculated about; and though the bulk of Nestroy's autograph manuscripts have survived, how they did so is another hair-raising story (see Gladt 1967: 11-21). Shortly after the First World War the heirs to Nestroy's estate offered a collection of them for sale. In the course of 1922 transcriptions were made by Adolf Hoffmann, working for the Viennese publishing house Anton Schroll & Co., which was about to launch a new edition. In 1923 the city of Vienna purchased the manuscripts on behalf of the Stadtbibliothek (now Wiener Stadt- und Landesbibliothek), but when Hoffmann's transcription was complete it emerged that the library had received only some two-thirds of the material promised, and that many of the manuscripts were incomplete. Whole pages had been cut into pieces as mementoes; and autograph corrections and addenda, of the kind that Nestroy frequently pinned on his manuscripts, had been unpinned and removed for the same purpose.

It was an unsatisfactory basis for the fifteen-volume *Sämtliche Werke* published by Schroll in the years 1924-30 under the joint editorship of Fritz Brukner and

Otto Rommel. The publication of this edition is part of one of the most striking phenomena in the cultural and intellectual life of Vienna in the years following the First World War, an upsurge of interest in local history and local cultural history, especially in the "Old Vienna" of the Biedermeier age — part of the reaction to the break-up of the Habsburg monarchy. Wilhelm Bietak published a study of the literature of the period (Bietak 1931), in which he defined the typical Biedermeier outlook as a resigned but not pessimistic acceptance of the reality of life as it is. A parody such as *Weder Lorbeerbaum noch Bettelstab* fits into the pattern in that Nestroy uses reality to show up the fanciful quality of the tragedy in the Holtei original (138); but elsewhere Bietak's normative approach leads him to draw unconvincing parallels between Nestroy's figures and those of other dramatists: Kern in *Der alte Mann mit der jungen Frau*, for example, is compared to Raimund's Rappelkopf (149). Nevertheless this conception of Nestroy as a Biedermeier author would live on into the 1940s (e.g. Bujak 1948).

The Nestroy edition was one of several ambitious editions of Viennese dramatists of the previous century published by Schroll in the 1920s, including a seventeen-volume set of Anzengruber, of which Rommel was one of the editors (1920-22), and a seven-volume set of Raimund, of which Brukner was one of the editors (1924-34). While Brukner's private collection of manuscripts was one of the bases of the Nestroy edition, the actual editorial work was done mainly by Rommel, with considerable input from Adolf Hoffmann until his death in 1928. Nestroy studies were to remain heavily dependent on this edition until the end of the 1970s; but although it contains all the comedies acknowledged by Rommel and Brukner as having certainly been written by Nestroy, it is editorially very inadequate. In some ways, indeed, it is even less satisfactory than the edition of 1890-91 (*CG*) because it aspires to the status of a historical and critical edition, and so to a textual authority which Chiavacci and Ganghofer did not claim.

To some extent, of course, it has — inevitably — been overtaken by events; our knowledge of Nestroy's sources, for example, has been steadily extended. But the deficiencies were there from the outset, and extend to the whole organization of the edition: the plays are divided into supposedly separate genres (including three volumes of "*Volksstücke*," a misleading term that is not authenticated by any surviving Nestroy manuscript). Breaking up the chronological order of writing or performance obscures the extent to which Nestroy's work underwent an organic development. The separation of "*Zauberspiele*" and "parodies" into discrete sections is misleading, an obstacle to perceiving the specifically *satirical* element common to both. Rommel tries to justify the choice of ten plays as *Volksstücke* by reference to their moral and didactic content in contrast to more trivial works by Nestroy's contemporaries (Rommel 1926: 563); but he has to concede that there are no formal grounds for the division. There are other deficiencies, too. Neither Nestroy's correspondence nor the early drama *Prinz Friedrich* is included. The documentation both of variants and of contemporary reception is incomplete, and the reproduction of reviews is extremely unreliable. (In view of these defects it is regrettable that the apparatus to the edition is still widely cited.) Even more important is the inaccuracy which which manuscripts are transcribed, both in the main text and in the variants: over and above simple misreadings, there are

damaging inconsistencies (sometimes spelling and endings are amended to fit
modern orthographical norms, at other times dialect endings are introduced
which are not in the manuscript), and material from separate manuscripts is not
always clearly distinguished.

The edition gave a significant boost to Nestroy studies in that it provided for
the first time a text of almost all of his work, with an apparatus of annotation and
bibliographical information; but its textual and methodological shortcomings
were increasingly to hamper serious Nestroy scholarship, the more so since (with
more or less revision) it formed the basis of all subsequent selected editions,
including Rommel's six-volume selection of 1948-49 (*GW*), until the launching
of the new historical and critical edition (*HKA*) in the late 1970s.

The final volume, however, brought a major contribution to scholarship, a
monograph by Rommel which was by far the most important study of Nestroy
so far (Rommel 1930). Its framework, established in the first section, is the history
of Viennese dialect comedy; Rommel locates Nestroy and Karl Carl in their
historical place in its development, and presents Nestroy's work as arising organically out of the Viennese tradition of popular theater (70-73). He traces the
vagaries of his critical reception and distils from contemporary accounts (not least
Gutt's reviews from 1844) an analysis of a development in his acting style, from
the aggressive power of his early years, based on grotesque effects, to a more
moderate, more "humorous" and realistic style in the main part of his career —
"Das Dämonische seiner Satire wird überwunden durch Humor" (190) — and
then to his return to more grotesque effects of caricature and sarcasm from the
mid-1850s (328-30). Rommel is concerned to relate this development in Nestroy's acting to his dramatic work, seeing the acting style of his "maturity" as
having "created" the major *Possen*, from *Die verhängnisvolle Faschingsnacht* to
Kampl (193). He characterizes Nestroy as a skeptic, dominated by his intellect
(231); the aggressiveness of his wit set him apart from all precursors (233-37).
This intellectual component motivated his adaptation of the local comedy that
he had inherited to the needs and spirit of a changing society: he transformed the
theatrical central figure from the shallow intrigant of comic tradition by adding
a new element of reflection both in solo scenes (monologues and *Couplets*) and in
dialogue (269).

Rommel's account is copiously documented throughout, and draws fully on
Nestroy's letters in Brukner's collection. Brukner would eventually publish a
separate edition of the letters (1938), which is now superseded (except in so far
as it remains the textual source for letters the manuscripts of which are now lost),
but which is still useful for the background documents Brukner prints from the
time of the 1848 revolution. A feature of particular interest in Rommel's monograph is the written and anecdotal evidence he assembles on the various contra-
dictory components of Nestroy's character and temperament in private life
(self-ironizing but passionate, shy but promiscuous, kindly but irascible) (206-31);
in particular he draws attention to Nestroy's well-documented anxiety about
thoughts of death (218-19). Rommel's interest is not merely biographical. He is
concerned to probe the psychological roots of Nestroy's wit. That Nestroy's

character warranted investigation as the foundation of his art had been argued in 1925 by Liegler, who had concluded that he was essentially irresolute and consequently took refuge behind "masks," finding on the stage a unique possibility, not available to him in private life, for self-expression (Liegler 1925b). This analysis, however, is still dependent on an over-simple equation between the dramatist and his characters, in that Liegler perceives his characterization as "self-irony," rooted in experience. Otto Stoessl too would look for connections with Nestroy's life in Weinberl's depiction in *Einen Jux will er sich machen* of his longing for escape from bourgeois norms (Stoessl 1935: 230). Rommel, less crudely, relates Nestroy's wit to a fundamentally "depressive" temperament (Rommel 1930: 280) — an analysis which is based partly on Friedrich Kaiser's account of Nestroy's (initially uneasy) relations with the younger comic actor Carl Treumann (227-30; see Kaiser 1870: 203), and which has not commanded universal agreement.

The most important feature of all in Rommel's monograph is the apparatus, which provides and annotates the fullest possible historical documentation of Nestroy's career. Much of the material had been previously published in newspapers but Rommel brought it together for the first time. The apparatus includes a list of Nestroy's roles, with the dates of his appearances (428-516), based partly on Nestroy's own notes and partly on a long run of theater-bills from Carl's company in Brukner's collection; contracts between Carl and Nestroy dating from 1835 and 1847 (561-64) and a standard contract dated 1837 between Carl and one of his house playwrights, Karl Haffner (542-48); and the full text of Nestroy's will, which he drew up in Graz in 1861 (618-22).

Rommel also gives the text of two sets of what he calls Nestroy's "aphorisms" (680-705). The term is misleading. What Nestroy kept was a store of witty formulations, most no doubt invented but some drawn from his reading (see Walla 1972: 73-76), which he numbered systematically and intended for incorporation in his manuscripts as they were needed. Rommel's choice of the term "aphorism" led to an overvaluation of their function, as when Joseph Gregor, for example, the first director of the Theater Collection (Theatersammlung) of the Austrian National Library in Vienna, argued that the dramatic form served Nestroy only as a framework for aphoristic utterance (Gregor 1943: 229). Nestroy's own heading over the longest set of these notes, reproduced by Rommel from the collection of Franz Trau, is "Reserve" (see *SW* 15: 680). This manuscript seems no longer to be extant, so that the 1930 text (*SW* 15: 681-703) is now the only record of it; but the Wiener Stadt- und Landesbibliothek possesses a further similar manuscript (see Gladt 1967: 96), on which Rommel drew in his later six-volume edition of 1948-49 in a further list of notes compiled from various manuscripts (*GW* 6: 577-81). As with all the texts in Rommel's editions, the transcription contains inaccuracies.

The publication of this documentary material falls outside the province of Nestroy criticism in the strict sense, but it is symptomatic of the steady advance in serious Nestroy scholarship. Indeed, the material in Rommel's monograph (though it all has to be checked in detail) is still an indispensable resource. Other important documents relating to the background of theater history were published by Franz Hadamowsky, who would eventually succeed Gregor as director of the Theatersammlung. One was a detailed summary of Nestroy's work as director of the Carltheater from 1854 to 1860, an important time which saw the death of Scholz, a growth in the prominence and influence of Carl Treumann, an increase in the number of one-act plays produced, and the introduction into the repertory of Offenbach operetta (Hadamowsky 1926). Eight years later Hadamowsky produced a catalogue of the holdings in the Theatersammlung of texts, including manuscripts, drawn from the stocks of the Theater in der Leopoldstadt and Carltheater, combined with a listing of the repertoire of the two theaters from 1781 to 1860 (Hadamowsky 1934). Though again there are inaccuracies in detail, this volume too is still a fundamental reference work.

How successful the fifteen-volume edition in particular was in stimulating further interest may be gauged from the appearance of the first popular study for the general reader (Forst de Battaglia 1932), which is based on the material in the edition. Unfortunately this monograph added up to no more than an introductory account and was rightly criticized as journalistic and ill-planned (Körner 1933). The author is concerned to stress the "seriousness" underlying Nestroy's work, including, for instance, *Das Mädl aus der Vorstadt*, which he describes as a subtly comic treatment of "very serious social questions" (Forst de Battaglia 1932: 65); and he sees Nestroy's greatest achievement as lying in his harnessing of his commanding linguistic artistry to the wisdom of his plays of ideas ("Thesenstücke" [97]). But the treatment of the examples quoted is uncritical, sweepingly positive verdicts on individual plays being given on what are basically ideological criteria — as, for instance, in the description of *Kampl* as a "masterpiece," despite the artifice of the construction, because of the humanity and clear-sightedness embodied in the title role (100).

A much more significant development was that Nestroy was beginning to be seen in a clearer historical perspective, in the context of the intellectual currents of his time — the perspective that had consistently eluded his contemporaries. The lapse of time since his death and the documentation provided in the fifteen-volume edition now worked together to allow a more objective view, and this development can be seen in a number of publications — some of them stimulated directly by the appearance of Rommel's edition, but all by figures connected with Karl Kraus's circle and influenced by him. Liegler presented Nestroy ("geistig ausgedrückt") as the destroyer of an outdated optimism; Friedell, defining him as undermining Romanticism, placed him together with Grabbe and Büchner; Stoessl described him as akin to Daumier in spirit (Liegler 1930: 5; Friedell 1932: 163-67; Stoessl 1935: 226).

One positive indication that Nestroy was also at last gaining academic respectability was the completion at the University of Kiel of a dissertation in which Max Bührmann undertook the first systematic investigation of the parodies (Bührmann 1933). This study is based mainly on material in the fifteen-volume edition (*SW*), and the disadvantages of Rommel's organization of plays by supposedly separate genres are reflected in Bührmann's selection of his material:

he concentrates on the plays in Volumes 3 and 4 of *SW*, leaving out two plays, *Der Zauberer Sulphur...* and *Der Kobold*, which — as he himself records (49) — were conceived as parodies of Raupach's *Robert der Teufel* and a ballet by Jules Perrot respectively (see Diehl 1969: 133-43; *HKA*: *Stücke 6*: 156-65; *Stücke 14*: 258-63) but which Brukner and Rommel classed as *Zauberspiele*. Bührmann's approach is by no means free from the influence of older critical literature; he still tends to take as authorial statements sentences or aperçus, such as Leicht's declaration of his aims in *Weder Lorbeerbaum noch Bettelstab* (96), lifted out of their dramatic context. But the whole structure of the dissertation proclaims an acceptance of the need to treat Nestroy with scholarly method. Bührmann distinguishes parody and travesty, outlines the history of parody on the Viennese popular stage, lists the roles Nestroy played in parodies by other dramatists, and discusses the well-documented elements of caricature and gesture in his acting that lent themselves to parodistic use; one of the distinctive features of the dissertation is the weight he places on the close link between Nestroy's acting and his work as a parodistic dramatist. He divides the parodies into three periods, corresponding to Rommel's division of Nestroy's acting into three periods (156-60), and discusses the relation of individual parodies to their sources and the theatrical circumstances that determined their genesis, that is, not only the roles for specific actors but also the timing of their production to exploit the exposure of the originals (160) — a calculation alluded to by Nestroy himself in an important letter of 1856 which we now know was written to Bauernfeld (see Hein 1987c: 43-46).

The Nestroy scholarship of the first third of the twentieth century has been systematically surveyed by Jürgen Hein in the journal *Wirkendes Wort* (Hein 1968). In retrospect, it is clearly a period of significant advances, notably Kraus's celebration of the range and depth of Nestroy's linguistic satire, and Rommel's controversial exploration of the psychological basis of his wit. What is still lacking at this stage is the kind of close interpretation of individual texts that abounded in the critical literature on established classics such as Goethe or Grillparzer. Oskar Katann's essay on *Der Zerrissene* (Katann 1932) may serve as an example: Katann is concerned not to look for the distinctive individual subtleties of the play but to bring out *typical* features of the genre, in this case defined as the "Charakterposse" (96). He describes all the characters as exaggerated "caricatures" (97), the satirical songs as expressing an authorial view (97), and the plot as being made up of conventional comic motifs (98). Like Forst de Battaglia (Forst de Battaglia 1932: 65), Katann looks no further for the theme of the play than that indicated by the title, the modish phenomenon of *Weltschmerz* (Katann 1932: 94); describing the central figure, Herr von Lips, as a "hysteric," who is enlightened and cured in the course of the action (95), he advances the play as proof that Nestroy has "positive ideals" (93). It is as though he were still fighting the battles of the previous century, still defending Nestroy against moralistic disapproval.

No significant interpretative literature emerged from Germany after the establishment of the Nazi régime in 1933. In Austria, however, there were two important publications on the brink of the *Anschluss*: one was Brukner's edition of letters (1938), the other a slim monograph by a younger Austrian scholar, Franz H. Mautner (b. 1902), which may be regarded as a distillation of the critical

literature of the whole period since 1912 (Mautner 1937). The text was also
printed as the introduction to Mautner's one-volume select edition which appeared the same year.

In an earlier article on the significance of wordplay in literature, Mautner had
already treated Nestroy (especially *Der Talisman*) as a central illustration of the
use of wordplay as a means of characterization, pointing to the contrast in
Nestroy's works between the central figures acted by Nestroy (whose grasp of
ambiguity, allowing them to play masterfully with language, is the basis of their
wit) and their helpless butts who seem at the mercy of language (Mautner 1931:
704-5). In his book, which presents Nestroy as the greatest satirist of the German
stage, and again centres on *Der Talisman* as the wittiest of his plays (Mautner
1937: 7), Mautner repeats the point about language as a means of characterization
and interprets the reflective wordplay in the roles of the central comic figures as
expressing the author's own judgments (48). He presents Nestroy's linguistic
artistry as lying at the creative heart of his work: "Nestroys Kunst ist im Innersten
Sprachkunst" (42-3). He not only illustrates the vividness of Nestroy's imagery
(44) but shows how satire itself arises out of the exploration of language, exposing
conventions that mask reality (47-48). The influence of Kraus on Mautner's
interpretation is marked, both in the central concern with language and in the
detail of his emphasis. He is concerned, for example, to reject the idea that *Der
Unbedeutende* shows Nestroy as a forerunner of Anzengruber (57); and two of the
plays he singles out for special praise are precisely the two of which Kraus had
published adaptations: he identifies *Der konfuse Zauberer* as the first play showing
Nestroy's distinctive linguistic skill (21), and points to subtle psychological effects
in *Die beiden Nachtwandler* (33).

The rise of Nestroy's reputation was also reflected in press reviews of new
productions: also in 1937, for example, Oskar Maurus Fontana celebrated his
"greatness" and "genius" as evidenced in *Der Talisman* (Fontana 1937). But in the
following a year the *Anschluss* brought serious interpretative engagement with
Nestroy to a halt in Austria (now known as the "Ostmark"), as Viennese dialect
comedy became "das ostmärkische Volksstück" (Gregor 1943: 227) and the
ideological jargon of the time penetrated almost all public discussion. The only
specialist publications of importance in the period of Nazi rule are those that could
steer clear of ideological issues by treating technical and factual questions: the
music in his plays (Bauer 1944), his early reception in Graz (Friess 1940-41), and
his sources (Wallner 1941). Wallner succeeded in identifying the sources of two
works, *Liebesgeschichten und Heiratssachen* and *"Nur keck!"*, in the contemporary
English theater: originals by John Poole and Dion Boucicault respectively. Wallner's treatment of his finds is, however, somewhat uncritical, especially in the way
he takes for granted the superiority of Nestroy's versions. Boucicault's *London
Assurance* was in fact the most accomplished original comedy that Nestroy ever
adapted (see *HKA: Stücke 34*: 120), and the records of the two plays in the theater
hardly support the case for the superiority of *"Nur keck!"*.

Like Grillparzer, Nestroy appealed to Nazi ideology as an example of autochthonic ("bodenständig") art, though stress on local Viennese qualities ran

counter to the emphasis on pan-German unity. The result was that while there was a marked increase in Nestroy performances in Vienna by comparison with the period 1930-38 (see Hüttner 1964), productions tended to play down his satirical bite. In 1937 Jura Soyfer could celebrate him as a radical, on the side of the exploited against the exploiters (Feder 1937); under the Nazis his works were regularly reduced to trivial theatrical romps conveying a mood of uncomplicated Biedermeier gaiety (see Obermaier 1987). The first-ever production of *"Nur keck!"* in the Wiener Bürgertheater in 1943 provides a well-documented example, the text having been adapted and modernized and the emphasis being placed on an effect of Biedermeier "humor" (Liebl 1943). Gregor too is concerned to stress "pure humor" as the aim even of *Judith und Holofernes* (Gregor 1943: 236).

The authentic Nestroy spirit was kept alive in Zürich, where a number of distinguished Austrian émigrés came together in the Zürcher Schauspielhaus and actors including Karl Paryla performed in Nestroy productions directed by Leopold Lindtberg, with updated *Couplet* texts by Hans Weigel. All these figures would return to Vienna after the war and play a prominent part in the second Nestroy revival.

4: The Postwar Boom

A: The Establishment of a "Classic"

After the Second World War there was an immediate upsurge of interest in Nestroy. In 1948-49 the firm of Schroll brought out a new six-volume edition by Otto Rommel (*GW*), which contained most of the best-known plays in a text based on that in the fifteen-volume *SW*, with some minor revisions. The first volume was prefaced by another long essay, in which, by comparison with Rommel's monograph of 1930, the emphasis is placed more firmly on the satirical impulse in Nestroy's work, and on the "aphorism" as the basic creative element in his writing (Rommel 1948: 158). The stress on satirical intention also characterizes an essay on Nestroy's songs in the final volume of the edition (Rommel 1949). This latter essay prefaces a full index of the satirical songs, which Rommel would subsequently supplement by further texts written by Nestroy for roles in plays by other dramatists (1955).

At the same time there was a sudden boom in productions in Viennese theaters. In the Nazi period Nestroy had been promoted as a representative of indigenous folk-culture; after the war, with the whole of German-speaking Europe liberated from the ideology of Nazism, he appealed as a radical satirist to newly opened left-wing theaters (in particular from 1948 onwards the Neues Theater in der Scala in the Russian sector of the city, where Karl Paryla, one of the great modern Nestroy actors, played in several productions after his return from Zürich). Since Austria was re-establishing its separate national identity, Nestroy (like Grillparzer) also appealed as one of the principal classics of a specifically Austrian tradition of theater. He had never taken firm root in the Burgtheater between the wars; in the early 1950s a new impetus was provided by the work of a young Munich director, Axel von Ambesser (1910-88), and of Leopold Lindtberg, another to have returned from Zürich (see Reichert 1957; Fontana 1962; Obermaier 1988a). The new popularity enjoyed by Nestroy in the theater quickly spread through the other German-speaking countries also, but its center remained in Vienna, where the climate was made all the more propitious by the return from exile of two distinguished critics, both disciples of Kraus, Hans Weigel (1908-1991) and Friedrich Torberg (1908-1979). Selected reviews by both would later find their way into collected editions (Weigel 1961; Torberg 1966: 183-202). Weigel's essays of this period include one of the most perceptive short introductions to Nestroy's work, written to commemorate the 150th anniversary of the dramatist's birth and stressing Austrian characteristics in his art and outlook (Weigel 1951); he also included a chapter in his book *Flucht vor der Größe*, presenting Nestroy as typically Austrian in being a great dramatist whose works were not great plays (Weigel is particularly dismissive of *Der böse Geist Lumpacivagabundus*, ever-popular but, he argues, lacking even in linguistic invention and satirical sharpness) but were constructed round roles designed to be played in the dialect theater (his "flight into the *Vorstadt*") — works in which, as Weigel puts it, Nestroy takes nothing seriously but his satire (Weigel 1960: 86).

It would be foolish to pretend that suddenly all the old prejudiced assumptions about Nestroy had melted away in a new dawn of universal insight. How tenaciously some of the old clichés lived on can be seen, for example, in a history of Austrian literature by Josef Nadler (1884-1963), whose treatment of literary history on a geographical and ethnic basis had enjoyed considerable authority since the inter-war years and who had been appointed to a chair at the University of Vienna in 1931. By comparison with Raimund's "poetic" qualities, Nestroy's work is presented by Nadler as negative, lacking all emotional depth and therefore not to be regarded as genuine imaginative literature ("*Dichtung*") at all (Nadler 1951: 311). It is a fine miniature example of the kind of misjudgment that inevitably follows if one applies inappropriate criteria, in this case those of a limited and old-fashioned conception of imaginative literature. Against this may be set what was in many ways a very positive assessment published the same year by the journalist Willy Haas (who had been born in Prague and was one of the many émigrés of the 1930s). Haas's essay was stimulated partly by the appearance of the six-volume edition (*GW*), partly by the publication of Rommel's monumental history of Viennese dialect comedy, the final chapter of which is devoted to Nestroy (Rommel 1952). Haas stresses the allusiveness and complexity of register in Nestroy's language, explaining these effects as arising out of his capacity both to parody material and also at the same time to absorb it. He also emphasizes the breadth of his perceptiveness, arguing that Wendelin's second song in *Höllenangst* (*GW* 5: 278-81) in effect forecasts both the Crimean War and the Schleswig crisis, and that the caricature of Holofernes in *Judith und Holofernes* anticipates the Nietzschean Superman.

Nevertheless, Haas's treatment of Nestroy's text is still methodologically primitive. For example, on the basis of another song from *Höllenangst*, Wendelin's defence of his "superstition" in the teeth of all "enlightenment" ("I lass' mir mein' Aberglaub'n / Durch ka Aufklärung raub'n" [*GW* 5: 306-8]), he denies that Nestroy was committed to enlightenment or can be said to satirize human stupidity (Haas 1952: 1086), an identification of author and role that discounts the specifically satirical effect of the song in its dramatic context. Or again, by declaring that Nestroy's concern was only to entertain, Haas in effect takes over the traditional ascription to him of the attitude of Leicht in *Weder Lorbeerbaum noch Bettelstab* (1084). The conclusion he draws is that it would be wrong to compare Nestroy with Shakespeare, who was not a (mere) craftsman of the theater and whose characteristic sense of creative poetic genius and belief in his own genius Nestroy lacks. This is an unproductive argument, based on Nestroy's constantly joking scepticism towards elevated pathos; that is, Haas's position assumes a fundamentally romantic conception of "genius" that is no more appropriate to the whole temper of Nestroy's work than Nadler's insistence on emotional force. Berger had put it better forty years earlier when arguing that Nestroy's creative abhorrence of untruth and artifice was evidence precisely of his sure feeling for the genuinely "poetic" (Berger 1912).

That old battles continued to be fought long after they had ceased to be live issues can also be seen in the revised version of Forst de Battaglia's monograph, the underlying aim of which is to show Nestroy's character as more complex than the traditional image of his "cynicism" by contrast with Raimund (Forst de Battaglia 1962: 76). Though there are some shrewd analyses of single sallies taken out of their dramatic context, there are few substantial new insights in this book; it is another piece of popularization, setting Nestroy's career in its theatrical and historical context, discussing his acting and language, summarizing his "philosophical outlook" as belonging essentially to the Biedermeier period, and finally assessing his distinctive "Austrianness."

The growing recognition of Nestroy's stature and importance and the increasing sophistication of critical approaches to his work are, however, reflected in the appearance not merely of well-rounded general introductions (Mautner 1963; Preisendanz 1969) but also of three books of considerable quality aimed at a wide readership. One, by Otto Basil (1901-83), is a chronological account in the popular series of illustrated monographs published by Rowohlt (Basil 1967). It has shrewd comments to make on many of the plays and is probably still the best biographical study available. Three years later a longer and very readable chronological account was published by a Viennese theater critic, Kurt Kahl (Kahl 1970). The third book, by Hans Weigel, gives accounts of a selection of plays, reflecting Weigel's long practical experience both as an adapter and as a theater critic, and is particularly notable for including in the central canon *Höllenangst*, a play that had hitherto been little regarded but which had enjoyed great success in a new production by Axel von Ambesser in the Theater in der Josefstadt in 1961 (Weigel 1972). All three of these books take Nestroy seriously, without the element of polemically defensive apologia characteristic of Forst de Battaglia's two monographs. This was also the time when the first monographs appeared in languages other than German, designed to provide scholarly introductions for a primarily academic readership and reflecting a growth in interest outside German-speaking Europe (Bauer 1965; Yates 1972; Destro 1972; Harding 1974). Clearly Nestroy was genuinely becoming accepted as a classic — a status that would finally be confirmed in the late 1980s when the firm of Reclam in Stuttgart launched a "basic library" (*Basisbibliothek*) of German literature since the mid-eighteenth century, a boxed set of twenty-five volumes drawn from their famous paperback "Universal-Bibliothek," and included a Nestroy text (*Der Talisman*) in the collection.

Looking back now on the rapid expansion of Nestroy studies that took place in the twenty-five years or so after 1950, it is striking how dependent most of the published work remained both on the research of Otto Rommel and on the interpretative stimulus of Karl Kraus. The vitality of the Kraus/Mautner tradition concentrating on Nestroy's language as the crucial creative element in his work is manifest in a number of publications, including a detailed analysis of specific linguistic devices by an East German scholar, Dagmar Gengnagel, which is especially indebted to Mautner (Gengangel 1962). The most important of the language-orientated studies is a monograph by Siegfried Brill, based on a Frankfurt dissertation (Brill 1967). Brill himself sums up his work as an explication of Kraus's description of Nestroy's work as "written acting" ("geschriebene Schauspielkunst" [151]). He presents a narrow conception of Nestroy's achievement, seeing his work as artistically successful only in its linguistic comedy: "Nur das eine, die Komödie der Sprache, gelingt: alles andere mißlingt" (181). This narrowness would be strongly criticized by other scholars (Hillach 1967; Herles 1974). In a sense the argument that since Nestroy is dead, the text is all that we are left with (Brill 1967: 9) is self-evidently right, and the intrinsic (literary) merits of the text are well worth defending: "[Nestroys] Werk kann als Literatur ohne Seitenblick auf den Komödianten bestehen" (226; see Walla 1991); but one weakness of Brill's study, which emerges strikingly when he is concerned with the "genesis" of Nestroy's linguistic comedy, is how little account he takes of the theatrical context. He is also uninterested in details of the social background: Nestroy's work, he argues, is related to society and the structure of society in so far as his *language* is determined by convention and reflects the society in which the convention is rooted (131). This approach is too restrictive: to ignore the specificity of historical events is to remove the allusive resonance of Nestroy's satire from its historical context. What Brill attempts, drawing examples mainly from *Der Talisman*, is a systematic classification of ten principal devices of linguistic comedy used by Nestroy. It is an over-rigid method but succeeds in bringing out both Nestroy's central concern to unmask clichés and also the functional complexity of his dialogue, where in a single speech elements of communication, comedy, and comment may be combined (134). It is this complexity of function which, as Brill observes, makes it dangerous to excerpt single sayings from their context and treat them either as personal "confessions" or as expressions of Nestroy's own opinion, not least his political opinion (102).

The influence of Kraus, which helped to shape perceptions of Nestroy for over half a century, has now itself passed into history, and a first attempt to survey it methodically was made by Helmut Rössler (Rössler 1981). Rössler traces the development of what he calls Kraus's campaign for establishing Nestroy as a new classic (28); he defines Nestroy's importance for Kraus as a satirical model and constant point of reference (33), a contrast to the moral and linguistic corruption of the press, and analyses the contrasting strategies underlying the two adaptations of Nestroy plays that Kraus undertook in the 1920s as a counter to the "Regietheater" of Max Reinhardt and others. Rössler is dependent on Kraus and Mautner in his reading of Nestroy; by the time his study (originally a Stuttgart dissertation) had appeared in print, the strongest criticism of Kraus's long hold over Nestroy criticism had also appeared. This criticism was mounted by Friedrich Sengle, who argues against exclusive concentration on Nestroy's language at the expense of the influence of practical traditions in the theater (Sengle 1980).

Whether or not under Kraus's influence, however, many of the studies that appeared in the 1960s and early 1970s (and there was a considerable flood of them) centered on aspects of Nestroy's linguistic wit. Christoph Kuhn, working from Nestroy's transformation of the traditional opening monologue of the central figure in Viennese dialect comedy, examined the importance of wit in the very design of Nestroy's plays (Kuhn 1966). Erwin J. Haeberle described him as the first public prosecutor of double standards in language, decoding the jargon of self-deception (Haeberle 1970). Alberto Destro, in a coherently argued and in my view insufficiently regarded monograph, defined the "intelligence" of the central figure (the Nestroy role) as the structural heart of his work (Destro 1972). Walter Jens wrote a brief analysis of a song written by Nestroy, not for one of his own plays, in the mid-1830s (*SW* 9: 176-77), expounding the density and and metaphorical richness of the language in an essentially lyrical mode (Jens 1975). Nestroy's influence on his successors in the popular theater, Kaiser and Anzengruber, was also examined explicitly in respect of his language (Yates 1968, 1972: 185-89).

The characteristic tension between wit and satire in Nestroy had been defined both by Rommel (Rommel 1930: 292-93) and by Kraus, whose formulation is that Nestroy's wit was not transfused into (moral) pathos but is set off against false pathos (Kraus 1912a: 13-14). Nestroy criticism contains many echoes of the eighteenth-century German conception of satire, which (by contrast with the traditional English emphasis on its corrective function) is steeped in moral and aesthetic idealism. Stoessl, for example, clearly draws his concept of comedy from Schiller (Stoessl 1935: 220). After the war, Herbert Eisenreich presents Nestroy as a realist about himself and the world, reflecting the concerns of his age from personal involvement in it, and consequently lacking the pathos of the true satirist (Eisenreich 1964); and the terminology of the Schillerian concept of satire is adopted by Jürgen Hein in the published version of his Cologne thesis (Hein 1970).

One of the problems facing critics trained in an idealist or realist tradition is the impossibility of treating Nestroy's comic figures as coherent autonomous characters. It is not just that comic drama always — generically — tends to deal in types, and that Nestroy takes this to an extreme of caricature: comparing the characterization in *Freiheit in Krähwinkel* with that in Kotzebue's *Die deutschen Kleinstädter*, Brill, for example, concludes that Nestroy "stretches type-characterization into the grotesque" ("Nestroy forciert die Typisierung ins Groteske" [Brill 1967: 100]). There is also the phenomenon that Weigel defines, in a memorable formulation, when he observes that most of Nestroy's sentences are set in invisible quotation marks: "Die meisten Sätze Nestroys stehen in unsichtbaren Anführungszeichen" (Weigel 1960: 93). That is, there is a disjunction between the wordplay of the dialogue, in which language itself is not merely the medium but also the subject of the comedy, and the roles of the characters in the plot. This leads Brill to observe, again of *Freiheit in Krähwinkel*, that Nestroy's language is too consciously controlled to express subjectivity; hence the "impossibility of identifying a character in a Nestroy play with what that character says" ("die Unmöglichkeit, eine Person im Nestroystück mit dem zu identifizieren, was sie sagt" [Brill 1967: 102]).

The most sustained attempt to work within categories drawn from eighteenth-century aesthetic theory while avoiding one-sidedness is Hein's adoption of the concept of play ("Spiel"), derived ultimately from Kant's *Critique of Aesthetic Judgment*. Hans Weigel had identified Nestroy's compulsive "playing," manifested most strongly in his wordplay, as the key to his artistic character (Weigel 1960: 94). Hein develops the idea further, focusing on the interaction of "play" and satire in Nestroy's work, the means (including various breaks in illusion on stage) by which satire, relating to the real world outside the fiction, is established within a comic fiction that is essentially a world of "play" (Hein 1970: 15-17), with the result that linguistic "play" itself contains the germs of satire (51): the two impetuses work together, both constantly inherent in the roles of the central figures. Hein places especial weight on the function of the solo scenes, in which reflective satirical songs (*Couplets*) are sung by central characters who function as intrigants within the fictive world (150) but who in the solo scenes step outside the action, so challenging the audience to make a connection between the fictional action and the real world outside the theater (117-18). This effect is exemplified in *Einen Jux will er sich machen* (154); and from the distinctive development of the *Couplets*, Hein dates Nestroy's attainment of the fully-fledged *Posse mit Gesang* to 1840 (92).

By the beginning of the 1970s pressure for a revision of the fifteen-volume *SW* was beginning to build up, and was not assuaged by new selections such as the three-volume "Insel-Nestroy" edited by Mautner (1970), a good edition with some emendations of Rommel's text, but still fundamentally based on *SW*. The inadequacies of *SW* were most forcefully demonstrated in books by Siegfried Diehl and Helmut Herles, both based on Frankfurt dissertations — two of a remarkable series of dissertations on Nestroy that emerged from Frankfurt, stimulated and supervised mainly by Paul Stöcklein.

Diehl's important study of Nestroy's early work (Diehl 1969) proved a seminal stimulus for the research of the next quarter-century — together with two other outstanding studies by Ansgar Hillach and Erich Joachim May (Hillach 1967; May 1975), it marked a decisive step in advancing Nestroy studies forward from the Rommel/Kraus era. From hitherto unpublished manuscripts Diehl provided substantial evidence of the need for a new edition. Nestroy's handwritten fair copy of *Der Zauberer Sulphur...*, for example, had been acquired by the Stadtbibliothek in 1925, a year after the volume of *SW* containing the play had appeared; Diehl's analysis demonstrates the satirical and parodistic character intended by Nestroy, which had been watered down by later adaptation. His study of the manuscripts of *Der konfuse Zauberer* broadens out into a comparison with *Der Tod am Hochzeitstage*, which he identifies as an earlier treatment of the same theme (96-131). Over and above his contribution to textual criticism, Diehl prompted a fundamental reassessment of Nestroy's development by challenging the customary critical neglect of most of his early work, in which Rommel, for example, had denied the presence of a serious satirical intention. He establishes the independent importance of the early work (a line that would later be fruitfully developed by Friedrich Walla) and shows ways in which it anticipates Nestroy's later writing both in technique and also in ideas and themes. This extends even to ideas in *Prinz Friedrich* that are later echoed in *Der Talisman* (28). A more general point is how Nestroy uses the supernatural world of theatrical convention as a symbol of an absurd world-order, so disturbing the surface of Biedermeier peacefulness (172-73): Diehl points forward to parallels in the post-1849 plays, including *Höllenangst*. How radically Diehl succeeded in revising the established view of the early plays and breaking down the distinction between them and Nestroy's later work— "Damit scheint mir die oft behauptete Trennung zwischen Früh- und Spätwerk endlich aufgehoben ... zu sein" (183) — may be gauged from a review summarizing the main thrust of his argument:

> Siegfried Diehl shows that the magic apparatus, so dear to the Viennese Volkstheater, becomes in the early Nestroy an instrument for social satire that represents the collapse of traditional values in Vienna in the nineteenth century. ... In *Der böse Geist Lumpazivagabundus* and the plays related to it ... Nestroy is not deliberately trying to break down Raimund's ideal world, but he is revealing the emptiness of the real world with its sentimentalities and superstitions: the breakdown of the magic apparatus is the corollary to all this. ... Ultimately the magic in Nestroy is pure theatrical fantasy, its function is parodistic, showing that "deeper meaning" can no longer be taken seriously. The social satire in the plays is directed against those who live as though the world were the plan of benign spirits while everything around them suggests that it isn't. (Barlow 1971: 88-89)

In his earliest work — including *Zwölf Mädchen in Uniform*, which Diehl claims to prove is an authentic Nestroy play (Diehl 1969: 182) — Nestroy does not use the conventions of the old *Zauberspiel* at all; but when he does adopt the form, it is, Diehl argues, in outright satire of the convention, "eine grundsätzliche Verspottung des Geisterwesens" (182). Diehl also draws from his analyses illustrations of Nestroy's modernity; in this respect his findings tie in with those of Martin Esslin, who had already pointed to Nestroy as anticipating the theater of the absurd, partly by his mastery of "linguistic absurdity," partly by his parody of pretentious drama (Esslin 1962: 241).

Herles's study of *Der Talisman* also argues the need for urgent revision of *SW*. He documents the genesis of what is probably Nestroy's finest play, following its development from the first sketch onwards. His study — which completely superseded an earlier Viennese dissertation comparing the same play with its source, the Parisian comedy *Bonaventure* (Tönz 1969) — provides the text of three hitherto unpublished manuscripts: the first outline, which is based closely on the French source (of which Herles also gives a complete transcription); Nestroy's scenario, which is divided into three acts and organized scene by scene, including provision for nearly all the musical numbers (a typical example of Nestroy's scenarios and, as Herles shows, a crucial stage not just in his construction of the plot but also in the imaginative generation of its language); and a complete draft of the parodistic medley (*Quodlibet*) in Act Three, where he lays stress on the comic and satiric effect of the music: "Bei Nestroy werden Hohn und Spott im Dreivierteltakt möglich" (Herles 1974: 175). Herles's discussion of various completed scenes concentrates on analysing Nestroy's technique, by comparison with that in *Bonaventure*, and he also attempts a comparison between *Der Talisman* and the extant fragments of a rival version by Joseph Kupelwieser. All the textual material is now available in the new critical edition (*HKA: Stücke 17/ii*); but Herles was the first to reveal the genesis of the play as a process of organic textual growth, showing that it is only in the final version that Nestroy's dialogue attains its distinctive variety of levels and range of perspectives. At the same time, by demonstrating the linguistic stimulus at work even when Nestroy was only drafting his scenario ("daß bei der sprachlichen Arbeit am *Talisman* entscheidende Impulse aus der Inszenierung im Szenarium stammen" [59]), Herles is able to show the need for attention not just to the finished text but to the dynamic process by which the theatrical language was generated ("den dynamischen Prozeß der Umwandlung von 'Schreibe' in eine komödiantische Sprache" [10]).

The other most important specialist publication of the late 1960s, again a reworked Frankfurt dissertation, is a monograph in which Ansgar Hillach explicates the effects of Nestroy's "dramatizing of comic dialogue": he isolates and analyses the different perspectives Nestroy attains by juxtaposing different levels of language and also by the gestures and postures prescribed in the stage directions. Hillach defines four principal "perspectives." One is that of the fictional character, who retains a consistent stance even if apparently within a break in the fictional action; this may itself take varying forms, from plotting to watchful reflectiveness. Another is that of the actor, a perspective that is often suggested by exclamatory histrionic language. That of the author — Hillach argues that more or less direct "authorial" statements *can* be sensed (Hillach 1967: 68) — is usually suggested by aphoristic points, which the audience may perceive as being directed at the public rather than as arising organically out of the dramatic situation. Finally the perspective of the audience itself may be evoked when the character speaks lines which seem distanced from the fiction and suggest the kind of reaction the audience themselves might have. In the most original part of his study, Hillach demonstrates the interplay of these various perspectives as they succeed one another in quick succession, interspersed with "restorations" of the fiction. Analysing scenes from *Frühere Verhältnisse* (76-84) and *Der Tod am Hochzeitstage* (88-101), he attempts a detailed breakdown of effects in performance as the linguistic register of the dialogue changes from character to character and indeed even within single speeches, creating that constant, and often rapid, change of perspective which is characteristic of Nestroy's work — not so much crude breaks in the illusion as rather what Herles would call transformations of the fiction, "Fiktionsverwandlungen" (Herles 1974: 138). Hillach argues that these changes of attitude or perspective — a complexity to be found especially in his later work (Hillach 1967: 135) — are a hallmark of Nestroy's characters, by comparison with those in traditional comedy: "Kennzeichen Nestroy'scher Figuren ist ... gerade der Wechsel verschiedener Haltungen, und als stärkster der zwischen einem Aufgehen in der Situation und einer fiktionsbrechenden Außensicht" (56).

Just how peculiar to Nestroy this effect is can be proved only by comparative analysis, which Hillach does not attempt (indeed, this is a gap that still needs to be filled). But the subtlety with which he brings out the shifts of registers marks another advance in the reading of Nestroy texts, and subsequent critics fail at their peril to take full account of his book. Michael A. Rogers, for example, in a

Cambridge dissertation, criticizes Hillach's aesthetics as "unnecessarily complicated" (Rogers 1976: 53). Rogers sees Nestroy's creative method as consisting in
combining and juxtaposing elements of theatricality and stock images of Viennese
life, achieving a novel effect of conscious conventionality: the central structural
principle of Nestroy's work, then, is its combination of discrete elements of
conventional theatrical style, verbal associations, and Viennese stock jokes. Rogers
would later develop this line in relation to specific *topoi*, e.g. Nestroy's treatment
of the social role of servants (Rogers 1985). The strength of his dissertation lies
in his recognition that verbal and theatrical elements work together. His analysis
of Nestroy's method as the "continual manipulation of discrete elements by means
of their associations" (Rogers 1976: 104) leads to a definition of Nestroy's satire
as being "concerned less with the individual details than with the pattern they
create, and the assumptions that lie behind them" (136); the comic world of
Nestroy's drama, built of conventional elements, reflects a conception of the real
world as correspondingly "theatrical," an acting-out of conventions. But the basic
claim that Nestroy works "with an extreme consciousness of convention (of which
the audience, if not at all times the characters, is permanently aware)" (169) runs
counter to the detailed analyses in Hillach. Rogers has continued in subsequent
essays to argue that Nestroy "is not operating with the reality of Vienna, but with
the image of that reality which the Viennese themselves accept" (Rogers 1978:
76). The obvious objection to this is that the notion of convention in the theater
is inseparable from the reaction of the audience, so that it is important to take
account of changes in the public and its expectations during a period of profound
social change. It is inherently restrictive to approach the problem of convention
by textual analysis, without analysing the nature and response of the audience —
a factor that might be linked with Hillach's "audience's perspective" ("Perspektive
des Zuschauers").

A few years before the new edition was launched, Mautner, who had
emigrated at the time of the annexation of Austria by Nazi Germany and who
ended his academic career as professor at Swarthmore College in Pennsylvania,
published a major new study, the culmination of his own engagement with Nestroy
for over forty years and at the same time a summation of Nestroy scholarship in
the first three decades after the end of the Second World War (Mautner 1974b).
It remains strongly influenced by Kraus in its interpretative approach and dependent on Rommel's editions for its documentation.

The book begins with a general introduction presenting Nestroy as a sceptic,
essentially a Vormärz Liberal in attitude, whose linguistic awareness is the most
individual quality in his comic style (27). The distinctive qualities of his art,
Mautner argues, include a combination of formal and intellectual "mannerism"
(86) with the use of popular forms and themes; an element of the grotesque, which
accords with Nestroy's view of mankind as "marionettes," victims of an unjust
Fate; and the importance of playfulness ("Spiel") as a creative impulse both in his
characteristic use of antithesis and in his satire — here Mautner takes up the
theme treated by Hein (Hein 1970). In Mautner's view, sheer delight in comic
invention is a far stronger component in Nestroy's creativity than any moral or
moralistic purpose (Mautner 1974b: 100).

The second and most important part of the book gives a chronological account of Nestroy's career, short sections of biographical narrative linking individual critical interpretations (some admittedly very short) of all the plays. In this account, *Der Tod am Hochzeitstage* emerges as a key work in Nestroy's early years, in which he begins to use language — as Karl Kraus would later — both as an object of comedy and at the same time as a means of social and cultural criticism (138). Mautner dates the "classical *Possen*," in which central figures are fundamentally benign ("gutherzig") and the language has a less "mannered Baroque" quality ("etwas weniger maniriert barocken Charakter" [223]), to the period 1839-1842, with *Der Talisman* the "classical *Posse*" *par excellence*.

The book is rounded off with a short account of the rediscovery of Nestroy in the twentieth century and an outline discussion of the "modernity" of his appeal. This takes up a thread in an earlier essay in which Mautner had stressed Nestroy's modernity and suggested connections with Dürrenmatt (*Theaterprobleme*) and Brecht (Mautner 1963). Other subsequent work on this theme includes a further exploration of the relationship between Nestroy and Brechtian theater by a Soviet scholar, G. S. Slobodkin, and more recently both a comparison between Nestroy and Horváth by Louise Adey Huish (Oxford), published under her maiden name (Slobodkin 1978; Adey 1989), and also a paper by Egon Schwarz which includes a brief account of *Der Talisman* as the very "prototype of comedy as allegory," deploying devices that belong to the "epic-panoramic" theater associated with Brecht (Schwarz 1991: 46).

In the first part of his 1974 monograph, Mautner gives a succinct summary of the technique and function of Nestroy's central comic figures — almost all of them rebels. Nestroy, he acknowledges, did not identify himself with the central role in his plays; rather, he established contact with the audience by breaking the fiction, stepping out of his "role" in the dramatic action. But both in the monologues and in ripostes within the dialogue he gave the central figure lines to deliver which express what he had to say about mankind and the world, lines rich in intellectual wordplay and aphorisms. In this way the function of the central figure is transformed into that of a *raisonneur*, who during his monologues and songs speaks directly to the public virtually all the time, and also does so to a large extent in the dialogue, which fits in with the dramatic situation and yet is only seemingly genuine dialogue ("Streckenweise aus der Handlung heraustretend, spricht er zum Publikum, im Monolog und Lied so gut wie ausschließlich, reichlichst aber auch im durchaus situationsgemäßen und dennoch nur scheinbaren Dialog" [51]). The difficulty experienced by Nestroy's own public is mirrored here, even compounded. Nestroy was at one and the same time a private individual, playwright, and star performer in his own plays. The critic has to distinguish between the separate functions. Mautner's analysis fails precisely to differentiate person and function. In the detailed interpretations of the second part in particular, the least convincing feature of his method is in consequence his repeated interpretation of the monologues and satirical songs of the central figures as vehicles for the dramatist's self-expression; so too in the first part he refers to what he takes to be Nestroy's "true feelings" (e.g. 90). A series of characters are taken as speaking for Nestroy: "Leicht becomes Nestroy," we are told of *Weder Lorbeerbaum noch*

Bettelstab ("Leicht wird Nestroy" [197]); and there are similar implications in the way he writes of "Lorenz-Nestroy" in *Die verhängnisvolle Faschingsnacht* or of "Vinzenz-Nestroy" in *Die beiden Herrn Söhne.*

Mautner's treatment of *Die beiden Herrn Söhne* shows the unclarity of his approach. On the one hand, referring to a speech in the third act of Nestroy's draft version (a passage actually deleted from the version performed), he affirms, quite arbitrarily, that the greater pathos characteristic of the language of the "good" cousin, Moritz, is "meant seriously" by Nestroy (263); on the other hand his keen appreciation of Nestroy's linguistic wit leads him to comment on the same passage as giving the impression of parody (67). Mautner himself observes that Nestroy's reputation as a cynic has resulted from his identification with such figures as Nebel in *Liebesgeschichten und Heiratssachen*; but is that more arbitrary than a definition of Nestroy as a "radical sceptic, good at heart," a "radikaler, aber herzensguter Skeptiker" (111)? Mautner supports his choice of the epithet "herzensgut" with an allusion to Nestroy's character in private life — a correlation that runs counter to all the often-observed disparities between Nestroy's (often tongue-tied) private character and his (aggressively fluent) theatrical persona.

B: The Major Advances

The progress of scholarship up to the early 1970s is charted in the second of Jürgen Hein's reports in *Wirkendes Wort* (Hein 1975), in an annotated bibliography by John Peroutka Bruckner (Bruckner 1973) which complements Hein's account, in a further study by Hein surveying the state of research in the whole field of Viennese dialect theater (Hein 1978), and in the long chapter on Nestroy in the final volume of Friedrich Sengle's *Biedermeierzeit* (Sengle 1980). Surveying the critical and scholarly literature of the 1960s and 1970s, over and above the specific interpretative angles adopted in the individual monographs and dissertations discussed above, it is possible to pick out five particularly significant developments which point forward to later advances.

First, there is less dependence on the kind of purely local focus that restricts Nestroy to specifically Viennese effects and connections. The strength of interest in local history and folklore after the First World War had left its mark on the Nestroy edition of the 1920s (*SW*) and the Anzengruber edition which Rommel also coedited in the early 1920s. Throughout his career, Rommel continued to concentrate on exploring continuities within what he presents as an essentially popular theatrical tradition; but this emphasis tends to deflect from the commercial character of the suburban theaters, which in fact, far from being peculiar to Vienna, were strictly comparable in repertory and organization to the commercial theaters in mid-nineteenth-century London and Paris.

It was possible, in fact, to take international comparisons back further. The whole theatrical life of Vienna in mid-century, with the creative tensions between the court and suburban theaters, provides a point of comparison with the public and private theaters of Shakespeare's London. Karl Kraus had suggested that there is a "Shakespearian" vividness in Nestroy's language (Kraus 1912a: 10); now the subtitle of Kahl's monograph (Kahl 1970) dubbed Nestroy the "Viennese Shakespeare," and at a more scholarly level Manfred Draudt, a Shakespeare specialist, undertook an extended comparison against the background of parallels between the theatrical life of Biedermeier Vienna and that of Elizabethan London (Draudt 1980).

The attack on the restrictively "local" approach was led by another Viennese scholar, Johann Hüttner, who shifted the emphasis of scholarly intention on to the financial and organizational practicalities of the theater, including specifically the importance of the box-office both for the individual performer and playwright and for the repertory (e.g. Hüttner 1977). The importance of commercial interests as a determining factor in the theater was also emphasized by Rio Preisner (Preisner 1972: 25), while in an influential East German study (originally a Leipzig dissertation) the theater historian Erich Joachim May set out to link Nestroy's work in the 1840s with production conditions as represented in its critical reception (May 1975). This book, which reflects a growing interest in the importance of the public in the theater (see Yates 1977), is a pioneering study of the reception of Nestroy's work. Though May's quotations of reviews are often inaccurate in detail, he effectively established the special importance of the critical climate for Nestroy's works, concentrating on the critical dispute in the press of the 1840s about rival genres, and arguing that the debate reflects political pressures building up in the run-up to the revolution. May's findings have subsequently been extended and modified as increasingly detailed attention has been paid to the press in Nestroy's Vienna (Obermaier 1991), to the critical criteria adopted by the reviewers of the time (Neuber 1987; Yates 1983-84, 1987), and to the debate about the notion of an idealizing *Volksstück* (Müller 1979; Yates 1985a; Hein 1989b).

A second development at this stage was a strong emphasis on the element of social and political criticism in Nestroy. It is typical of the intellectual climate of the 1960s that critics with a Marxist background or influenced by Marxist thinking were prominent in concentrating on this thrust in Nestroy's work. As a satirist Nestroy thought in cosmic terms, presenting society as governed by principles of providential and inescapable injustice; the danger in swinging away from reducing him to an author of trivial farces and turning him into a serious social critic was that this would lead to a new kind of one-sidedness, and Mautner was sharp in pointing out the danger (Mautner 1973). The tendency can already be observed at its most uncritical in Martin Greiner's treatment of the "genius" and clarity of Nestroy's social perceptions as revealed in *Freiheit in Krähwinkel* (Greiner 1954: 46-47), a discussion in which not aesthetic or dramatic effect but revolutionary commitment forms the central criterion. The play is deemed a "positive" reaction to the revolution but not as revolutionary in spirit, because Nestroy lacked the reformist optimism of the true revolutionary: he affirms the revolution, so Greiner argues, but mocks the half-heartedness of the revolutionaries and their (bourgeois) lack of conviction, which he himself shared and which condemned them to failure. Nearly twenty years later Horst Denkler still saw the same play as a satirical presentation of the inadequacies of the revolutionaries in relation to the ideas and ideals of revolution (Denkler 1973: 351). Denkler interprets Nestroy simply as an oppositional writer — one, indeed, whose work helped to bring the revolution of 1848 into being (179). He reads *Zu ebener Erde und erster Stock* as a demonstration of the "basic laws" of capitalist exploitation (188) and reduces Nestroy's work as a whole to a cumulative satire of a political stasis founded on the social stagnation of the Biedermeier period, the kind of attitude of complaisant resignation summed up in Schnoferl's description of passive "Sarkasmus-Languissance" (*SW* 11: 12), with the Biedermeier ideal of "contentment" ("Zufriedenheit") exposed as a "surrogate" (*Eisenbahnheiraten* II,9; *HKA*: *Stücke 20*: 131), a consolation for material disappointment (186).

A similar left-wing bias informs a two-volume selection published in the East German "Bibliothek deutscher Klassiker" (1966), in which the weight falls heavily on plays of overtly social and political moment, including not only *Der Unbedeutende, Freiheit in Krähwinkel*, and *Judith und Holofernes* but also *Der Schützling* and *Der alte Mann mit der jungen Frau*. The Introduction by Paul Reimann is consciously slanted in a way different from that of "reactionary" scholarship in Western Europe: Reimann distorts Nestroy's ironical social satire into a sharp note of social criticism, interprets *Das Mädl aus der Vorstadt* (which is not one of the texts included) as evidence of his awareness of the growing exploitation of the "proletariat" in Vienna, and presents *Freiheit in Krähwinkel* as an attack on the forces of reaction and the cowardice of the liberal bourgeoisie in face of the threat from the heroic revolutionary workers (Reimann 1966: xxi-xxii).

Much more subtle studies were published by two other scholars with an East European Marxist background. Ernst Fischer commemorated the centenary of Nestroy's death in 1962 with a substantial essay in which Nestroy's satire of the complacent materialism of the bourgeoisie — Fischer sees this as the reason for the rejection of *Eine Wohnung ist zu vermieten*, the public having been provoked by satire of their own attitudes (Fischer 1962: 458) — is embedded in a convincing account of Nestroy's career against the background of Austrian economic history. In a monograph by Rio Preisner, *Eine Wohnung ist zu vermieten* plays a still more central part. Preisner relates Nestroy's work to the intellectual climate and social conditions of his day, and — in effect following a line of approach suggested by Liegler (Liegler 1930: 4-5) — identifies as a dominant type of the period the small-minded philistine, on which Nestroy based the central character, Gundlhuber (22). The loss of traditional values which in Preisner's analysis was characteristic of the intellectual climate produced an alienation reflected in Nestroy's creation of what Preisner calls the "tragic *Posse*" (34), comedy presenting a world peopled by human marionettes (36). Thus Weinberl's urge to escape into his adventures in *Einen Jux will er sich machen* is a dramatic enactment of his discontent with the restricting norms of bourgeois materialism, an escape doomed to failure as his adventures turn to nightmare. Preisner sees the play as symptomatic of the impending revolution, its direct relevance to the climate of the 1840s accounting for its immediate success (96-97). He traces his reading of Nestroy's work through a chronological account of his career, the new genre of the "tragic *Posse*" being achieved in 1835 in *Zu ebener Erde und erster Stock* (82) and culminating in *Der Talisman* (92); a stronger political element marks the plays written around 1848, with Nestroy then returning in his last years to the mode of the "tragic *Posse*." Preisner's study met with predictable objections on ideological grounds: it was "seriously marred by a rigidly socio-political approach and the accompanying tendency to interpret Nestroy's philosophy only in those terms" (Corriher 1979: 164). But it provided a stimulatingly radical rethinking of Nestroy's work, not least in the weight it placed on *Eine Wohnung ist zu vermieten* and *Gegen Torheit gibt es kein Mittel*, both hitherto little regarded, as plays of central importance; and the frequency with which it continues to be quoted shows that it is standing the test of time well.

The first study in English of Nestroy's treatment of the events of 1848-49 is only a short introduction, but gives a balanced account of his critical independence, summing him up as "an enlightened conservative with strong liberal tendencies" (Barraclough 1960: 256-57). The interest in his social and political satire is widely reflected in West European and North American publications at this time; but in general, direct connections between the comic fiction and the real world outside the theater are more cautiously made than in East European and Marxist publications. In particular a critic such as Reinhard Urbach, approaching Nestroy from the viewpoint of theatrical convention, is thoroughly alive to the artifice of the relationship between comedy and reality. He presents Nestroy's work as a turning-point in Viennese comedy, in that in Nestroy, criticism of reality and satire of language grow apart: his comedy is a social fiction, played in a satirical stage-Vienna ("in einem satirischen Kulissen-Wien" [Urbach 1973: 118]), with chance the fundamental principle driving the action and determining the form: "Der Zufall ist mehr als Thema der Komödien Nestroys, er ist auch ihr dramaturgisches Prinzip" (121). So too Karl-Heinz Stierle, considering *Einen Jux will er sich machen* in particular, sees the very structures of bourgeois normality comically distanced in a world in which chance reigns supreme (Stierle 1976: 264). Of course, this effect is a device propitious to social criticism: that Weinberl's urge to escape into his adventures is implicitly critical of social norms and expressive of a symptomatic lack of fulfilment was widely recognized (e.g. Apel 1979; Ahrens 1982: 238). Alois Eder, assessing the evidential value of Nestroy's satire for the social history of pre-industrial Austria, defines his satirical intentions as "diagnostic" (as opposed to "therapeutic") and relates the divergence of opinions on the political tendency of the satire precisely to these "diagnostic" intentions; but he too concedes that most evidential weight has to be placed on the incidental details worked in by Nestroy in his adaptations of borrowed and conventional plots (Eder 1973a).

The most substantial contributions at this stage to the evaluation of the political implications of Nestroy's work are studies of single works. Henri Plard published an essay on *Judith und Holofernes*, considering its parodistic force — it is, he argues, distinguished from Nestroy's other parodies as a piece of essentially literary criticism, a parody of a specific style as opposed to *travestie* in the French sense (Plard 1963: 405) — but also stressing its political character as a reflection of the 1848 siege and the attitude of the Viennese population, with both anti-clerical and anti-Semitic tendencies suggested (409-13). So too Fischer had drawn a parallel between Holofernes and Windischgrätz (Fischer 1962: 468); and

Judith und Holofernes was one of two plays, the other being *Freiheit in Krähwinkel*, treated by John McKenzie, of the University of Exeter, in essays expounding the detailed relation of Nestroy's text to the historical background, his strategic "conjoining of farce and political satire" (McKenzie 1973, 1980). In the same period Urs Helmensdorfer published an analysis of *Der alte Mann mit der jungen Frau* in relation to Nestroy's other plays of the years 1847-49. Helmensdorfer stresses the relative mildness of the satire in the play, confirmation that it is inappropriate to see Nestroy as an aggressive radical. But though his essay is subtitled "Nestroy's Political Testament," his discussion is not narrowly focused on the question of the play's political import; he too concentrates on the mechanics of its construction, in this case the linking of the political theme with the "personal" action centring on Kern, the "old man" (Helmensdorfer 1974).

Thirdly, perhaps in consequence of the opening-out of perspectives beyond the stereotyped image handed down from the nineteenth century, there was a renewed interest in Nestroy's personality. The seminal publication in this respect was an essay by the Swiss Germanist Peter von Matt (Zürich), which was to become very influential in later reassessments (Matt 1976). The starting-point of the essay is a report (recorded in Rommel 1930: 218-19) that during his visit to Paris in 1857 Nestroy collapsed when seeing an oil painting by Charles Müller depicting the last roll-call of victims of the Reign of Terror (*Girondistes*), including, in the centre of the picture, André Chénier. The painting had first been exhibited at the salon of 1850, and though its ostensible subject is the French Revolution, Matt argues that to Nestroy its immediate associations were with 1848. Matt also quotes Nestroy's will with its admission of his fear of being buried alive and his stipulation that his coffin must not be nailed down. In Müller's picture, Matt argues, he may have glimpsed in a foreground figure bidding farewell to his wife and daughter a likeness of himself.

The anecdote about Nestroy's reaction to the Müller painting had also been touched on by Paul Schick (Schick 1956: 205). Fear of death, Schick argues, is a characteristic feature of the satirical mind (203), whose typical uncompromising clarity he illustrates from *Der Talisman*, where Titus describes his dead father as the "Verweser seiner selbst" (*HKA: Stücke 17/i*: 50) (209). Death is indeed ever-present in Nestroy's work, as in the melancholy reflection of the bricklayer Dominik Hauskatz in the first act of *Die Papiere des Teufels* that he can hear the grass growing under which he will one day be buried ("Ich hör' schon das Gras wachsen, in welches ich beißen werd'" [*SW* 11: 272]). The critical aggression of the satirist, Schick argues, is linked to an attachment to life (212-13) which is reflected in the plays in such figures as Gottlieb Herb in *Der Schützling*, who shrinks from suicide (I,6; I,13); one of the satirist's supreme weapons is to condemn an opponent symbolically to death, as in Nestroy's letter of 18 February 1849 to Saphir, in which Saphir is treated ironically as a pitiable "nullity" ("Nichtigkeit" [*HKA: Briefe*: 84-87]).

But whereas Schick's eye is on archetypal reactions in satirists in general, Peter von Matt is concerned with Nestroy alone, in the context of his age, and his essay amounts to an interpretation of Nestroy's whole perception of life. He presents him as having lived a life constantly on the edge of life-and-death panic, both in his amours and in the political pressures of a mid-nineteenth-century Austria which was in effect a police state. This condition of panic is reflected in the urgency with which the farcical misadventures in his plays are conducted, and is linked also to the clarity with which he perceives the insecurity of a once stable society suddenly in flux (Matt 1976). The note of fearful insecurity in Nestroy's plays had been noticed in yet another Frankfurt dissertation, that by Günther Boege, Titus in *Der Talisman* being compared with Büchner's Leonce (Boege 1968: 46); but Peter von Matt broadens the point out into a coherent reading of Nestroy's mind. Unfortunately this outstanding essay is not easy of access, but its importance was publicized when its ideas were used as the focal point of an exhibition mounted in Vienna to mark the 125th anniversary of Nestroy's death (see Hüttner 1987: 16).

Fourthly, the seed sown by earlier essayists such as Liegler, Friedell, and Stoessl began to bear fruit in that Nestroy's work was increasingly considered in a context wider than that of the dialect stage, so that scholarship began to be more receptive to its implications in the context of cultural history and the history of ideas, including the growing climate of political dissent characteristic of the literature of the 1840s (Seeba 1975; Baur 1981; Häusler 1987). Thus Roger Bauer's wide-ranging study of the development of Viennese drama out of the traditions and world-view of the Baroque and the Josephinian Enlightenment includes three chapters on Nestroy, in which Nestroy's burlesques of the *Zauberspiel* are seen as a disenchanted satire not just of the genre but of the whole notion of a providential world-order on which the genre essentially rested (Bauer 1965: 191). This rejection of a providential transcendental order is in Bauer's analysis the fundamental recurrent theme underlying Nestroy's *oeuvre* (251-53), which conspicuously informs both the sharp social satire of *Liebesgeschichten und Heiratssachen* in the early 1840s (219-20) and the rebellious attack on the very notion of Providence in the first act of *Höllenangst* (239-40). The link with the Baroque was subsequently explored by Ruprecht Wimmer, who defines the essence of Nestroy's work as lying in a secularization of allegorical elements derived from Baroque and Jesuit theater tradition. The early *Zauberspiele* present comic variations on inherited allegorical devices, with Nestroy creating a comic disjunction between language and allegorical context; in his later plays, the allegorization is absorbed into the language, with contemporary idiom, including everyday metaphor, used to subvert traditional values (Wimmer 1982).

A particularly important contribution to the art of reading Nestroy's satire, and specifically his treatment of political material, was published by Hinrich C. Seeba, who set out to establish the connections between Nestroy's satire and the intellectual and political climate of the 1840s. *Freiheit in Krähwinkel* emerges from his investigation as a satire on the language of the idealistic libertarianism of the time (Anastasius Grün, Bauernfeld, etc.); the illusions of the liberals are reflected in the quality of the "liberty" achieved in Krähwinkel, which suggests the discrepancy between libertarian rhetoric and reality. The review-like structure of the play is not a symptom of disengagement or indifference but a consequence of the illusions embedded in the libertarian rhetoric (Seeba 1975). A similar point is put rather differently by Peter Pütz, who also likens the structure to that of a review and relates it to the even-handedness with which Nestroy examines liberty in practice (Pütz 1977: 186). Seeba points out that the very name of Nestroy's poet "Sperling" suggests the satirical reference to the poets of the Vormärz (Seeba 1975: 145); and the awareness he stimulates of the allusive (and often double-edged) resonances in the language of the play allows a far more sophisticated and balanced interpretation than the one-sided and generally literalist readings of critics like Greiner and Denkler.

The widest-ranging example of the increasing willingness to study Nestroy in relation to the whole cultural context of his time is the account by Sengle (Sengle 1980), who treats him as one of the major figures of the Biedermeier age in German-speaking Europe as a whole. By contrast with the approach adopted by Bietak and others in the 1930s and 1940s (Bietak 1931; Bujak 1948), Sengle's awareness of an intellectual continuity deriving from the eighteenth century and his emphasis on the importance of oppositional writing allow him to place Nestroy securely in context beside Büchner and Heine, without falling into simplistic concentration on his social criticism.

Even in terms of the history of drama, Nestroy was now being seen in a wider framework. Earlier, Friedell had made the connection with Büchner and Grabbe. Boege too pursues the comparison with Büchner in particular (Boege 1968: 45-47) and identifies Nestroy, together with Büchner and Grabbe, as one of the fathers of modern European drama — a bold claim (355). Diehl similarly sees Nestroy standing to the traditional popular theater as Heine did to the Romantics (Diehl 1969: 174). Preisner, on the other hand, tries to draw out his aesthetic conservatism, as manifested, for example, in his parodying of romantic pathos in the theater, and in his parodies of romantic operas (Preisner 1972: 25-26), a conservatism which Preisner sees as being paralleled at the social and political level in his satire of contemporary faith in progress and in his repeated depiction of human incorrigibility from Knieriem to Gundlhuber, the unteachable Simplicius Berg in *Gegen Torheit gibt es kein Mittel*, and Heugeig'n in *Lady und Schneider* (28-29). In not proclaiming any ideology, so Preisner argues, Nestroy is set apart from bourgeois norms (34); and he quotes Salerl's saying in *Zu ebener Erde und erster Stock* that one must take the world as it is and not as it might be (*SW* 6: 19). Knieriem even rejects the whole pretence of bourgeois norms, and Nestroy's fidelity to reality is further illustrated in his satirical and ironic presentation of the conventions of marriage (Preisner 1972: 29-31). In the same year Helmut Arntzen published an essay interpreting *Judith und Holofernes* as a rejection not just of Hebbel's tragedy but, through the medium of parody, of the intellectual corruption of his age (Arntzen 1972).

A related widening of critical perspectives may be seen in studies by Bruno Hannemann and Kurt Corriher, arising out of dissertations submitted at the University of California, Berkeley and the University of North Carolina at Chapel Hill respectively. Both look at the philosophical implications of Nestroy's plays. Recognizing what has been called "the ruthless scepticism that runs throughout Nestroy's work" (Yates 1972: 78), Corriher defines Nestroy's philosophy as one of "rational scepticism" (Corriher 1981: 29); his characters struggle to affirm identity, clinging to hope in the teeth of their conviction that existence is pointless, and recurrently recognizing that they are at the mercy of arbitrary external forces, to which Nestroy gives the name "Fate" (Corriher 1979, 1981). The weakness of Corriher's analysis lies in his simplistic assumption that Nestroy's central characters often "function as a mouthpiece for their creator" (Corriher 1981: 28) and that in particular Lips, the central figure in *Der Zerrissene*, can be treated as "a key figure in interpreting Nestroy's world view" (Corriher 1979: 161). The parallel with Büchner is drawn briefly but not pursued; Hannemann, by contrast, setting out to challenge Nestroy's elevation to the status of a classic, poses the critical question "How good is Nestroy?" in an attempt to clarify his position in a explicitly historical context (Hannemann 1977: 1). Arguing from the way the shortcomings of the world as it is are blamed on "Fate," Hannemann defines the structure of Nestroy's work as an escape into metaphysics: "So könnte man die Genese der Nestroyschen Posse als die Geburt der Komödie aus dem Geiste der Metaphysik bezeichnen" (113). The subtitle of *Zu ebener Erde und erster Stock oder Die Launen des Glücks* is, he argues, indicative: a potentially explosive social theme, the contrast between rich and poor, is reduced to a matter of metaphysical caprice, the social question sidestepped (103). This is perhaps, he concedes, a consequence of the constant pressure of the censorship laws; but the effect is that the basis of human misery is not sought in human society but is projected onto a metaphysical lottery — a Baroque concept — over which mankind has no control (46). Hannemann stresses the continuing influence of Enlightenment thought in Nestroy's conception of human life as the pursuit of happiness (52) and the reluctance of his figures to accept the world as an unalterable creation (47): they are characteristically rebels against the injustice of a "Fate" characterized, in a long draft monologue intended for *Höllenangst*, as a "bureaucrat" (*SW* 5: 708). But as rebels they are also social outsiders, their typical note one of defeatist fatalism (Hannemann 1977: 123). Hannemann see Nestroy's art, then, as being in the final analysis nihilistic, his aphoristically aggressive wit an "aestheticizing of despair" (153).

Finally, perhaps the most important advance at this stage was an increased interest in Nestroy's methods of working and the practicalities of the conditions in which he worked. These included the constraints imposed by strict censorship, whose workings have still been only patchily documented (see Hüttner 1980a; Breuer 1982); a survey of the available sources and of Nestroy's developing reactions to the censor was undertaken by Herles, and the effects of the reimposition of censorship after the revolution were reassessed by Günter Berghaus (Herles 1973a; Berghaus 1977: 238-39). Considerable leaps forward were also made on the music in Nestroy's work. In his monograph on Raimund and Nestroy, which seems from internal evidence not to have been revised later than the early 1960s, Laurence V. Harding could include only a brief and rather general description of its character and importance (Harding 1974: 217-27), defining it as serving "to underscore the wit of [Nestroy's] dialogues and the idiosyncrasies of his characters" (227): more precise assessment became possible only once the surviving music was catalogued by Ernst Hilmar, now director of the music collection in the Wiener Stadt- und Landesbibliothek (Hilmar 1972), while Peter

Branscombe, defining a turning-point in Nestroy's use of music in 1842 and relating it to a specifically satirical intention (Branscombe 1976: 168-71), was able to demonstrate from details of the size of theater orchestras that the decline in the musical element of popular comedy in the 1840s was not a result of a reduction of facilities due to economic pressures (517-23). There was also further work on the critical reception of Nestroy's plays as a reflection of the tastes and ideas of the time (Eder 1973b; May 1975); on the history of Nestroy productions after his death (Hüttner 1964); and on reassessing his choice and treatment of his sources.

In focusing attention on the sources Boege was again in the vanguard. His dissertation investigates the influence of the form and content of Nestroy's sources on his adaptations, concentrating on three plays based on different kinds of sources: *Die verhängnisvolle Faschingsnacht*, *Der Unbedeutende*, and *Judith und Holofernes*. He poses the question whether Nestroy in effect reduces his borrowed material to a common denominator in the *Posse* form (Boege 1968: 44), and concludes that in the rare cases where he chooses more elevated literary sources they are not given fundamentally different treatment (352). In Boege's analysis, what Nestroy least criticizes or parodies is a trivial quality in the *structure* of his sources (56); that his own plays are not trivial is due to the dramatic relation he establishes between the central figures with their disillusioning intellect and the conventional framework in which they are set (354). That he took over substantial parts of his sources, even for central scenes of his adaptations, is in Boege's view due to practical exigency, his need to create roles at speed (57); the different intentions in his adaptations show especially in the prominence and the distinctive diction of the central figures (349).

Another dissertation that probed Nestroy's use of his sources was a Viennese one by Friedrich Walla (Walla 1972). This investigates various elements in Nestroy's dramatic technique (the nuts and bolts of his writing, as it were), and some of the findings are developed in later articles (e.g. Walla 1981b, 1986). An important feature of the dissertation is the attention given to Nestroy's collections of aphoristic formulations and their deployment in the plays from 1844 onwards. Among Walla's discoveries is the fact that Nestroy drew at least the germ of ideas for some of these formulations from *Martin Chuzzlewit* and used them as early as 1845 in *Die beiden Herrn Söhne*, three years before his full-scale dramatic adaptation of the novel, *Die Anverwandten* (Walla 1972: 75-76). His use of literary sources in this way is a further indication that even the pithiest formulations in his plays are far from being expressions of a personal viewpoint (126).

Nestroy's transformation of his sources is a form of "creative adaptation" (Yates 1972: 120-48) — a term that has found wide acceptance (e.g. Bauer 1976, Aust 1991). One suggestion put forward in the early 1970s that has continued to attract attention is that Nestroy worked best when adapting sources that were not complex and rich in their own comedy, as *Martin Chuzzlewit* is, but "sources that allowed him to work creatively, filling out his material with new comic life," so that "the most suitable sources were simpler, offering mere foundations on which Nestroy's critical imagination could build: the kind of trivial comedy he could transform with his satire, or a piece of pretentious or sentimental work such as he could virtually parody" (Yates 1972: 132). Walla reaches a similar conclusion in his comments on *Die Anverwandten*, a play in which the process of adaptation is short in genuine inventiveness (Walla 1972: 73).

All these problems bear centrally on the revaluation and interpretation of Nestroy's work. They could be identified on the basis of the outdated *SW*; but for their solution fuller and much more dependable evidence was needed, which could be supplied only by a completely new edition.

5: Edition and Discovery

In the mid-1970s a Viennese publishing firm, Jugend und Volk Verlag, committed itself to producing a major new edition, designed both to update the fifteen-volume *SW* and to remedy its deficiencies. The new edition was launched in the first instance under the general editorship of Jürgen Hein and Johann Hüttner (this editorial team was later enlarged). The first two volumes both appeared in 1977. They were an illustrated catalogue of portraits of Nestroy both in private life and on stage, *Nestroy im Bild*, based on material compiled by Heinrich Schwarz, and an edition of his letters, edited by the current director of the manuscript collection in the Wiener Stadt- und Landesbibliothek, Walter Obermaier (*HKA: Briefe*); this superseded the smaller collection edited by Fritz Brukner (1938). In the early years the edition was fortunate to have the committed support of an experienced writer, Helmut Leiter (1926-90), who was principal editor (*Cheflektor*) in the firm. Since 1979 the dramatic works have steadily been appearing, and by the autumn of 1992 the following seventeen volumes of *Stücke* had been published: 1, 5-6, 7/i, 7/ii, 12-14, 17/i, 18/i, 19-21, and 31-34. At that point nearly two-fifths of Nestroy's plays were already available in the new edition, and with volumes now appearing with increasing speed, the half-way mark should be reached in 1995.

Another significant development at about the same time was the launching by the International Nestroy Society of the journal *Nestroyana*, the first issue of which appeared in 1979. It was designed as an organ for publishing material relating not only to Nestroy but also to the Viennese tradition of dialect comedy in general. Its survival in its early years owed a great deal to the energy and dedication of Karl Zimmel, the Honorary Secretary of the International Nestroy Society, and it is now established as an indispensable forum for critical and interpretative discussion of Nestroy's work and career. It is also an important adjunct to the edition, in that corrections and amendments and also new finds (including acquisitions of manuscripts by the Wiener Stadt- und Landesbibliothek) are published in its pages.

The most important advance in our knowledge and understanding of Nestroy in the last quarter of a century undoubtedly lies in the text of the new edition. The first volume of plays to appear (*Stücke 1*) included the early drama *Prinz Friedrich*, which the fifteen-volume edition (*SW*) omitted because it is not a dialect comedy. (Other texts not printed by Rommel will include *Die zusammengestoppelte Komödie* in *Stücke 16*.) In contrast to *SW*, the plays are organized in chronological order, which allows the progression of Nestroy's work to be seen clearly in relation both to the changing theatrical context and to developments in the social background. The advantage of this is particularly clear for the evaluation of texts placed by Rommel among the so-called "*Volksstücke*," such as *Glück, Mißbrauch und Rückkehr* (now in *HKA: Stücke 14*). It also allows new light to be shed on a well-known comedy such as *Liebesgeschichten und Heiratssachen*, which Jürgen Hein interprets in *Stücke 19* as reflecting aspects of Vormärz society, its lukewarm reception related to the fact that it was competing with Nestroy's own major successes of the previous three years. Above all, the new edition establishes a text which is based as far as possible on autograph manuscripts and which is designed to come as close as possible to the authentic text completed by Nestroy for the première of each play. A large number of textual emendations have been made; and significant divergences in separate manuscripts are clearly shown. The issues and principles involved have been expounded by each of the editors of the first twelve volumes of plays to appear in the new edition (most recently Hein 1989a, 1994).

The presentation of the material in the new edition has benefited from the increasing interest in the practicalities of work in the nineteenth-century commercial theater; and the edition in turn has stimulated further interest in this area and contributed to the development of greater insight into Nestroy's working methods, the whole organic process of the genesis of a play (see Yates 1985b; Hein 1991a, 1994). To appreciate the principles on which his plays are constructed, Nestroy scholarship needs to take into account at every step the day-to-day constraints of the commercial theater. As Nestroy's preparatory notes and drafts show, his plays had to be planned round the specific actors at his disposal. They also involved close collaboration with his composers — for most of his career the fertile Adolf Müller (1801-86), whose autograph scores survive in the music collection of the Wiener Stadt- und Landesbibliothek. Under the financially tight régime of Karl Carl he had to avoid the need for expensive scenery (Hüttner 1981). And the most irksome source of constant pressure was the supervision of texts by the official censor. The interplay of these factors, which make up the whole framework of his creative work, is reflected in the mechanics of his writing, a process of detailed planning, drafting, and polishing (see the summary in Hein 1990: 103-4).

There are plays for which manuscripts have survived documenting practically every stage of this process. In the volume *Stücke 34*, for example, the genesis of *"Nur keck!"* is traced from its inception in Nestroy's notes on a contemporary version of Molière's *L'Étourdi* onwards, up to and including his autograph fair copy of his final text (in this case not quite complete). *Stücke 31* presents an almost complete documentation of the genesis of *Kampl* from Nestroy's early notes up to the final draft on which his fair copy must have been based. There is also very full documentation of the genesis of *Eisenbahnheiraten*; in this case Nestroy's notes do not start earlier than the scenario, but most of the translation that he used of his French source, a fairly free version prepared by a minor dramatist, Gustav Zerffi, has survived in manuscript together with Nestroy's annotation and is reproduced in full (*Stücke 20*: 393-429). In the case of *Der Talisman*, Nestroy sketched an outline translation himself (*Stücke 17/i*: 188-201).

The significance of all this material for our understanding and interpretation of Nestroy's work can best be illustrated by outlining how the material in the new edition (or collected by scholars working on individual volumes) illuminates some of the factors bearing on the conception and completion of a text. I shall concentrate on three examples: his choice of his source; the documentation of his preparatory notes and drafts; and his reactions to the institution of censorship.

The edition attempts to provide full documentation of Nestroy's sources and the use he made of them. The editor of the volume *Stücke 7/i*, Friedrich Walla, identifies and reprints the main source for *Das Verlobungsfest im Feenreiche* and *Die Gleichheit der Jahre*, K. G. Prätzel's story "Die Schloßmamsell." Other sources, not newly discovered but made newly accessible by being reproduced in facsimile, include those of *Der Talisman* (*Stücke 17/1*), *Einen Jux will er sich machen* (*Stücke 18/i*), *Liebesgeschichten und Heiratssachen* (*Stücke 19*), *Eisenbahnheiraten* (*Stücke 20*), and *Der Zerrissene* (*Stücke 21*). Work in progress on other volumes has stimulated further discoveries: by the end of 1992 the number of plays for which the source is still unknown had been reduced by three. One of the plays concerned is *Gegen Torheit gibt es kein Mittel*, which has been shown to be based on a novel by the prolific French writer Paul de Kock (1793-1871), *Ni jamais ni toujours* (1835) — the second Kock novel to be adapted by Nestroy in just over a year and a half (Adey Huish 1992a). As in his adaptation of *La Maison blanche* in *Glück, Mißbrauch und Rückkehr*, it is not possible to establish for certain whether Nestroy used the French original or the German translation, which appeared in 1837, since "he borrows the broad outlines of plot and incident rather than specific turns of phrase" (618). In this case the adaptation was less successful, partly as a result of the inherent difficulties of transforming a novel into a *Posse*, which have been discussed by Hugo Aust in relation to *Kampl* (Aust 1991). But Nestroy's reasons for trying to capitalize on the success of a popular French novel are not far to seek:

> De Kock's worldliness and the absence of moralizing in his novel were clearly attractive to a writer who was constrained to write within the tradition of the Viennese dialect theatre but who shared few of its moral assumptions. The elegant intrigues, the titillating eroticism, and the exuberant comic episodes to be found in *Ni jamais ni toujours* provided ready-made material for a playwright who was always writing against the clock. (Adey Huish 1992a: 624)

The two other plays concerned are late ones, *Heimliches Geld, heimliche Liebe*, which we now know to have been based on a popular French novel of the mid-1840s, *Au jour le jour* by Frédéric Soulié (Walter 1986), and *Frühere Verhält-nisse*, which was based quite closely on a one-act farce by Emil Pohl, *Ein melancholischer Hausknecht oder Alte Bekanntschaften*; a complete transcription of the Pohl text has been published in *Nestroyana* (Hein 1989-90; Tutschka 1989-90). Pohl's play is the first Nestroy source to be identified that was not available to Nestroy as a printed text: it had flopped in the Wallner-Theater in Berlin (it had only three performances there) and must have been supplied to him in manuscript by a theatrical agency. In addition to these finds it has been established beyond reasonable doubt that *Lady und Schneider* derives directly or indirectly from Eugène Sue's novel *Les Mystères de Paris* (1843); whether from the novel itself or from one of its many imitations and adaptations remains to be discovered (McKenzie 1991).

The finds themselves are, of course, only the raw material of interpretative scholarship. Where critical advances have been made is in close discussion of Nestroy's procedures in adapting his sources. In respect of the French sources, which are the most numerous, this is reflected not only in the new edition but also in a number of articles (Wimmer 1986; Doering 1988; Aust 1991; Schneilin 1991), in one monograph (Doering 1992), and in an edition of *Höllenangst* (Hein 1987b) in which the relation of Nestroy's text to his source is set out in tabular form, as in volumes *Stücke 17/i* and *Stücke 19-21*. There has also been work on the strategy underlying Nestroy's adaptation of English sources (Walla 1981c; Yates 1991a), and happily all three of the plays he based on contemporary English comedies have already appeared in the new edition: *Einen Jux will er sich machen* (*Stücke 18/1*); *Liebesgeschichten und Heiratssachen* (*Stücke 19*); and *"Nur keck!"* (*Stücke 34*). There is no evidence that he had much English; and how often he worked directly from French originals is not yet known. Against the Zerffi translation he used when preparing *Eisenbahnheiraten* must be set his own (even freer) translation of another French *comédie-vaudeville* which forms a preparatory stage of his work on *Das Mädl aus der Vorstadt*, and which has been edited by Susan Doering (Doering 1992: 156-284). Both of the French originals were by well-known Parisian playwrights, Charles-Victor Varin being one of the collaborators in both cases.

One striking feature of recent discussion is that whereas once it tended to be taken for granted that Nestroy's adaptations are infinitely superior to his sources, at least to contemporary comedies from Paris or London (e.g. Rommel's notes in *SW*; also Wallner 1941), this assumption has increasingly been questioned (e.g. Haida 1991; Adey Huish 1992a). There is growing recognition not only that some of the originals are works of quality but also that one of his motives for adaptation could be the time-honored wish to cash in on a proven success, a process of popularization rather than genuinely creative adaptation; this point has been made persuasively by Peter Haida about *Die Papiere des Teufels* (Haida 1991).

Another focus of critical discussion has been the relation of *Häuptling Abendwind* to Parisian operetta. Nestroy's source is Offenbach's one-act operetta *Vent du soir* (a work that in turn goes back to the subject-matter of *Robinson Crusoe* and Chateaubriand's *Atala*), and his adaptation injects the material with satire of modern civilization, reflected in the "savages" of the *dramatis personae* (see Obermaier 1984; Spohr 1985, 1989). The manuscripts of the musical arrangement prepared for the 1862 production appear to have been destroyed in the Kai-Theater fire in 1863, but a useful new edition of Offenbach's score has been published in a piano reduction, with Nestroy's text (Spohr 1990).

Nestroy's procedure in adapting his sources followed a broadly consistent pattern. After various preliminary notes picking out salient motifs and themes, he would draft one or more scenarios, often with frequent reference to the original from which he was working (see Hein 1991a). In the course of this process his conception of his characters would develop, from names or types borrowed from the original to identification in terms of the actor who would play the role (Nestroy, Scholz, Treumann, etc.), to the fictional type-name that would appear in the *dramatis personae*. Nestroy usually divided his paper vertically, writing his consecutive text — whether a scenario or a full version of his final text — on one half of a sheet and using the other half (sometimes two out of three columns) not only for amendments and additions but also, at each stage of his work, for jotting down ideas and snatches of dialogue. He generally wrote in pencil, with many abbreviations and corrections, and his early notes and drafts are often extremely difficult to decipher, as has been illustrated in the new edition in various facsimiles (e.g. *Stücke 19*: 263; *Stücke 31*: 517). His final scenario would characteristically set out a detailed outline of the entire play, which he would cross out scene by scene as he completed his full draft version; the new edition has already made available for the first time the text of a number of these detailed scenarios for plays of the early 1840s (*Einen Jux will er sich machen, Liebesgeschichten und Heiratssachen, Nur Ruhe!*, and *Eisenbahnheiraten*). It was not unknown for the design of a play to be changed at a later stage, and this too would be planned with painstaking care. In *"Nur keck!"*, for example, two scenarios, the second very detailed, were followed by an equally detailed "schedule of planned changes" ("Plan-Aenderungs-Programm" [*Stücke 34*: 182-86]). The dialogue, too, was subjected to careful revision; this has been most fully documented by Hugo Aust in his edition of *Kampl*, in which the draft version of a large proportion of the play is given in full (*Stücke 31*: 289-366) — a monumental labor of transcription which demonstrates the extent of the work Nestroy invested in the detail of his texts. At the final stage of revision this would extend, as for example in *"Nur keck!"*, to minute alterations to endings and inflections, differentiating the linguistic registers of individual figures (*Stücke 34*: 190-96).

The battle with the censor is less fully documented, since the copy-manu-scripts submitted to the authorities survive only for some plays. Nevertheless it constitutes an equally important factor in the later stages of the completion of a text for performance. A play such as *Der Zerrissene*, for example, was completed in the spring of 1844, at exactly the same time as Heine was writing *Deutschland. Ein Wintermärchen*: no less than Heine in a different medium, Nestroy and his fellow-dramatists had to devise a working strategy to get round the censorship problem. The censor would require the deletion of anything that might have a socially unsettling effect: any sexual *double-entendre* he noticed; any phrasing into which a political meaning might be read; and any formulation that might offend the sensibilities of the church. In the new edition, words and phrases expunged by the censor have so far been given in full in the volumes *Stücke 1, 6, 7/i, 7/ii, 13,* and *17/i*. The censor's approval could involve considerable eleventh-hour altera-tions: in the case of *Das Haus der Temperamente*, for example, conditional approval was given on 11 November 1837, and the première followed five days later. There was therefore a considerable degree of self-censorship; playwrights had to work within the bounds of what was permitted. There was also a system of provisional adaptation in detail, preparing in advance for the (predictable) objections of the official censor: passages of which the censor might be expected to disapprove were not crossed out but scored through with thin rings, and variants entered in above the line (see Hüttner 1980c, 1980d). Friedrich Walla has analysed the whole process of censorship and pre-censorship as evidenced in the plays already covered in the new edition (*Stücke 7/ii*: 315-23; Walla 1989, 1994). Nestroy usually entered precautionary variants himself in his autograph manuscript; these were copied into the manuscript submitted to the censor and it seems that often, if not always, the original passages were covertly reinstated in performance. (This can be deduced from the way deleted formulations reappear in later theater manuscripts.)

A final external influence that is being documented in the new edition is the critical reception of the plays. This documentation is being attempted comprehensively only in respect of the premières, but reviews by Müller and Gutt from Nestroy's appearances in Prague have been reprinted as well (see also Theobald 1992); in the case of *Einen Jux will er sich machen* a more general account is given of the early reception of the play outside Vienna (*Stücke 18/1*: 139-51); for *Kampl* too reviews of Nestroy's appearances in Berlin are given (*Stücke 31*: 189-95); and for *Der Talisman* the whole history of the play's reception up to the Second World War is surveyed in outline (*Stücke 17/i*: 115-83).

That Nestroy took account of the demands of his audiences has long been accepted: Mautner, for instance, points out that the luxuriant growth of wordplay in the later plays is probably connected directly to the expectations of the theater public in the 1840s and 1850s (Mautner 1974b: 82). The publication of so much material (much of it hitherto unknown) revealing the pressures exerted by the critics has prompted inquiry both into the consistency of the lines taken by the main reviewing journals (Obermaier 1991) and into the effect of the press reception of successive plays in determining the development of Nestroy's writing and in influencing the evolution of his form of the *Posse mit Gesang* in the late 1830s (see Yates 1985b, 1987, 1988a).

The complex picture that emerges of Nestroy's work is reflected in an exemplary interpretation by Jürgen Hein of a single play, *Der Zerrissene*. This essay takes account of all the factors bearing on the composition of the play and demonstrates the complexity of approach necessary when dealing with a Nestroy text (Hein 1988a). It provides a concise and informative introduction not only to Nestroy's technique in mid-career but also to the critical cruxes associated with interpretation and evaluation, including Nestroy's treatment of his source, the characteristic interplay of linguistic registers in his dialogue, and the significance of the critical reception. It is a clear demonstration of the new understanding in detail which the new edition has helped to generate and which in turn informs the most recent Nestroy criticism.

6: Cruxes of Modern Criticism

The way authors are perceived by non-specialists inevitably lags behind the current state of research. Even in a study published in 1992 and claiming both to serve an introductory function and to add to specialist understanding of Nestroy, Leicht's satirically phrased words about writing to provide profitable entertainment rather than aspiring to literary laurels can *still* be quoted as corresponding to Nestroy's perception of himself (Cersowsky 1992: 44). And as for publications aimed rather at the general public, one recent essay uses not only Leicht's speech but also Fabian Strick's equally overworked statement of his scepticism about human motivation, working both into an "imaginary conversation," and putting them into the mouth of Nestroy himself (Kaiser 1991).

It is no doubt asking a lot of publishers and editors of journals and monograph series to expect them to be in touch with current research in every corner of their subject; but certainly in the case of Nestroy, as Friedrich Walla has rightly lamented, work continues to get published which should not have been allowed to see the light of day (Walla 1991). It is invidious to give specific examples; just two may serve to illustrate the point.

Ulrich Scheck's study of *Judith und Holofernes*, originally a Master's dissertation at the University of Waterloo (Canada), shows one typical weakness, that of going over old ground. The thesis Scheck advances is, in my view, unconvincing; to argue, as he does, that the play does not contain strictly "parodistic" material directed critically against Hebbel is to apply criteria that are inappropriate to Nestroy's strategy and so to impose an arbitrary disqualification on a work which in its treatment of Holofernes is acknowledged to be the outstanding piece of critical parody in German, "das Meisterwerk kritischer Parodie in der deutschen Literatur" (Mautner 1963: 400). But that is just a matter of judgment. What is dated about the study is that much of it is taken up not just with summarizing the views of past scholars (a disease endemic in postgraduate dissertations) but with a descriptive account of correspondences and divergencies between the two plays — ground that has been covered over and over again (Scheck 1981). It is a competent dissertation for a Master's degree; but to accept it as a research publication was a mistake. My second example is an essay, arising out of a dissertation at the University of Indiana, by Joe Reese, on the relationship of *Der Zerrissene* to its source. The essay was published in 1990, five years after the appearance of the play in the critical edition (*HKA: Stücke 21*), but refers neither to that volume nor to any critical literature published since 1975. The inadequacy of the research behind this article is given away in the opening assertions, both inaccurate, that "the area of source comparison" (one of the central strengths of the new edition) has "remained somewhat unexplored" and that Rommel's edition "lists all of the sources" (Reese 1990: 55). Reese accepts an assertion written in 1972 to the effect that there is a shortage of historical and critical material on French popular drama of the mid-nineteenth century (56), ignoring publications since then, and defends *Der Zerrissene* against a criticism which was already recognized as being based on a misreading (Yates 1979: 43). There is no need to dwell longer on the article, which a knowledgeable editor or editorial board would have rejected; its acceptance exemplifies the gap that exists between dated perceptions rooted largely in the Rommel era and the understanding that has developed in the last decade and a half, not on the basis of modish theories but as a result of factual research and new documentation. The material available on *Der Zerrissene* includes not only a number of articles, which are summarized in the new edition, but also a comprehensive analysis by Jürgen Hein of the relation of the play to its source (*HKA: Stücke 21*: 120-41).

In view of this gap in awareness, it may be helpful to conclude with an indication of where the main thrust of productive Nestroy scholarship is now directed — not in an attempt to provide any kind of *Forschungsbericht* (see rather Hein 1990; Walla 1991; Yates 1993a) but rather to suggest the areas of insight that may lie behind the next advances in critical appreciation, as the new edition continues to appear and its predecessors are wholly superseded.

First, the structures and strategies of Nestroy's writing are increasingly illuminated by new insights into the working environment of the mid-nineteenth-century commercial theater and by growing recognition of the commercial factors bearing on Nestroy's work. These have been explored in a number of important essays by Johann Hüttner (e.g. Hüttner 1977, 1979). One result has been a revaluation of what is now seen as an exaggerated concentration in earlier criticism on the various genres of *comedy* in the dialect theater; it is necessary to allow more fully for the popularity in Nestroy's time — in Vienna as in London and Paris — of pieces of essentially melodramatic character (Hüttner 1980b, 1985). As well as providing Nestroy with sources for a series of plots in the 1830s and 1840s, the Paris theater exercised further direct influence on the repertory of the Viennese dialect theaters from the early 1850s through the operetta (see Obermaier 1988b). The means by which that influence was transmitted in Nestroy's time (translations, journals, agents, and so on) have been surveyed by Susan Doering (Doering 1992). Recognition of the many links and parallels between the Viennese suburban theaters and comparable theaters of entertainment in London and Paris means that by contrast with the traditional emphasis on "*popular* theater," with its rather sentimental overtones of folksiness, it is no longer justifiable to reduce the theatrical life of mid-nineteenth-century Vienna to a narrowly autochthonic stage tradition, a unique example of cosy local continuity (Hüttner 1986). Thanks not least to Hüttner's influential research, Nestroy's work is increasingly being treated in the context of the international theater of his time, as a number of recent essays confirm (e.g. Bauer 1990; Valentin 1991).

This international perspective further enhances the growing willingness, already discussed, to view Nestroy in the context of the wider intellectual and cultural climate of his time. Where once the roots of Viennese dialect comedy used always to be traced back to Austrian Baroque theater, he is now regarded essentially as an anti-Romantic (Münz 1988, taking up a point made by Friedell 1931: 167), who not only had links with contemporary intellectual currents in Austria (Baur 1981; Doering 1987) but also had affinities with the movement of ideas in German-speaking Europe as a whole (Sengle 1980; Haida 1987; Mills 1990). A natural corollary of these wider perspectives is that a start has been made on comparative studies: Nestroy's work has been compared not only with that of Heine but also with that of non-German contemporaries such as Boucicault and Labiche — appropriate comparisons since he adapted Boucicault's best-known comedy, *London Assurance*, in *"Nur keck!"* and played the role of Thomas Haserl in an version of Labiche's *Un Chapeau de paille d'Italie* (1851), adapting the part himself for performance (see Haida 1987 on Heine; Yates 1988a: 105-7 on Boucicault; Koppen 1982 and Doering 1992: 13-14 on Labiche). Looking forward in time, there have also been discussions of his affinities with Horváth, of possible "echoes" of *Der Schützling* in Wittgenstein, and of the contrast between Nestroy and Schnitzler in their treatment of the same social problem (Adey 1989 on Horváth; Barker 1986 on Wittgenstein; Yates 1990 on Schnitzler). Most of these comparisons merit further, more detailed examination; the article on Nestroy and Schnitzler, for example, fails to do justice to the satirical force of *Das Mädl aus der Vorstadt*: the party arranged in Act Two serves, as elsewhere in Nestroy (see Häusler 1991), as a metaphor for sensual indulgence, preserving the thrust of social criticism while not offending against the letter of the censorship laws. Or again, the parallels between Nestroy and Horváth in their critical manipulation of language are striking: the point is particularly well taken that in both, the "characters virtually all make love in the language of literature" (Adey 1989: 112); on the other hand, the degree of continuity between the dialect theater of the mid-nineteenth century and the revival of the so-called "Volksstück" in the twentieth can in my view be overstated (see Yates 1985a). There is, then, a need for further comparisons, especially with comic dramatists; Nestroy criticism has too often been content to describe Nestroy's distinctive effects (the contrasts in linguistic registers, for instance, or the interplay of satire and "play") without establishing to what extent they have parallels elsewhere in international comedy, in particular in comedy with equally deep roots in theatrical practice.

In some respects, documentation of Nestroy's work in the theater has continued to be improved. Records that have been mined include the diary for 1835 of his friend Ernst Stainhauser, later financial controller of the Carltheater under his direction (Obermaier 1982, 1985); we now have fuller information too on the guest appearances in Prague, Berlin, Graz, and other cities which took him away from Vienna in the summer (Obermaier 1984-85; Neuber 1987: 182-202). The pressures of working for a commercial theater, dependent on audience approval, with strict censorship in operation, imposed severe constraints. Hüttner rightly points out that Nestroy's greatness as a satirist lies in his capacity to overcome such constraints (Hüttner 1981: 155); and the corollary of that is that proper appreciation of his achievement requires understanding of the whole complex of strategies he adopted during his construction and revision of his plays. Detailed analysis has been devoted to practical features of his technique such as his use of quotation and self-quotation, the re-use of material from his own earlier plays, or the use of type-names (Hein 1987a; Walla 1981b, 1986). Among the wide range of dramatic devices he deployed, the most significant are those that show how the very structure of his plays is governed by a satirical intention: for example, the parodistic and satiric function of the characteristic "epic" quality in his dramatic technique (Münz 1988); his use of theatrical imagery and the metaphor of theater (Hein 1983a); the function of money, the core of materialist society, as the driving force in the dramatic action (Aust 1989); or his adaptation of the traditional happy ending of comedy, in keeping with the utopian idealism implicit in much satire (see Yates 1988b; Hein 1984-85; Münz 1988).

The question has also been asked whether Nestroy's world-view and especially his style betray the influence of his educational background. The question was raised in different ways both by Günter Berghaus and by Wolfgang Neuber (Berghaus 1982; Neuber 1987), the latter's book entitled *Nestroys Rhetorik* being based on a Viennese dissertation approved in 1980. Neuber accepts that interpretation needs to take into account the full historical context: Nestroy's effects need to be related not just to the context of the Viennese dialect theaters but to the wider cultural and intellectual climate of his times. The main part of the book, however, is a discussion of Nestroy's work in relation to a handbook, *Institutio ad eloquentiam*, that was in use in schools when he was a pupil: the dramatic *oeuvre* is approached as "rhetoric put into practice" ("praktizierte Rhetorik"), traditional rhetoric seen not merely as providing devices for attaining specific aesthetic effects but also as an overarching structural principle in the genesis of the plays ("als übergreifendes Strukturprinzip der Genese des Theaterstückes" [50]). This argument proved controversial. Over and above queries regarding details of emphasis and interpretation, two principal objections were raised. First, Neuber's exposition of rhetorical principles was seen as being insufficiently related to the aesthetics of the particular theatrical genres in which Nestroy was working, so producing a one-sided approach (Hein 1988c). Secondly, it was argued that the concepts and terms of rhetorical teaching were stretched by Neuber beyond the province of rhetoric proper into stage gesture and scenic effects, and so finished up as meaning no more than intended theatrical effects ("Wirkungsintention") (Yates 1988c). Neuber defended himself against the latter criticism by arguing that his use of the term is consistent with modern theory (Neuber 1991: 103); the counter-argument to that must be that the modernity of a fashionable theory is no methodological justification if it obscures rather than illuminating the subject under discussion. In fact Neuber's willingness to consider not just linguistic devices but different dimensions of theatrical performance working together is a strength of his approach; but credit for making the decisive breakthrough in that direction goes to Hillach, whose influence, together with that of May, Neuber acknowledges (Neuber 1987: 53). A stronger case for the influence of a specific kind of rhetorical tradition, that of the Baroque sermon, has been made by Maria Kastl (Kastl 1991), while Peter Cersowsky has explored another intellectual influence from the Baroque period, that of neo-Stoicism and specifically of neo-Stoic conceptions of virtue, culminating in the reappearance of Lips in the final act of *Der Zerrissene* as "Lipsius redivivus" (*HKA: Stücke 21*: 88), which he persuasively interprets as an allusive reminiscence of the seventeenth-century neo-Stoic philosopher Justus Lipsius (Cersowsky 1992: 110). This argument genuinely broadens our perceptions of Nestroy's intellectual heritage and marks an important step forward in the interpretation of so allusive a writer. The detailed annotation in the new edition underlines the breadth of allusion Nestroy works into his texts, reminiscences of Shakespeare, Goethe, Schiller, and Adolf Müllner and of contemporaries from Grillparzer to Scott and Sue. This network of allusion gives Nestroy's plays a highly literary quality that is most unusual in a dramatist working for performance in the commercial theater.

Detailed work on his methods has both stimulated and been informed by further investigation of the reception of his work. The weight placed on this factor derives from the recognition of Nestroy's reaction to press criticism. In 1847, reviewing *Der Schützling*, F. V. Schindler proclaimed that if Nestroy was now leading the way in developing a more positive form of popular drama, this was because he had been persuaded and reformed by the critics: "Kurz Nestroy ist durch die Kritik ein Anderer geworden und zwar zu seinem Vortheile" (Schindler 1847). The claim is exaggerated; but Nestroy's letters contain ample evidence that he took note of reviews by critics such as Bäuerle, Franz Wiest, and Joseph Tuvora, and there is good reason to believe that his choice of material and genre was at least sometimes influenced by his reaction to press criticism (see Yates 1987). The documentation of contemporary reviews in the new edition has made it possible to draw together the criteria applied by the critics in Vienna, and to follow the debate about the *Volksstück* as it developed from the late 1830s to the eve of the revolution (see Yates 1983-84, 1985a, 1993b). For the sake of completeness, I should also mention that where previously his reception outside Vienna had been the subject only of brief studies relating mainly to his acting in Graz and Frankfurt (Friess 1940-41; Herles 1969, 1973b), a start has also been made on fuller documentation of the reception of his plays in Berlin, Munich, and Prague (Theobald 1990; Adey Huish 1992b; Theobald 1992; see also *HKA: Stücke 17/i, 18/i, 31* on the reception of *Der Talisman, Einen Jux will er sich machen,* and *Kampl*). All this material helps underpin our appreciation of the climate of opinion in which Nestroy worked and the conditions he had to take into account.

The most restrictive external determinant was, of course, censorship. Though the working of the censorship laws prevented open satirical attacks on specific institutions and public personalities, Nestroy's plays abound in allusions to places and events, and the editorial responsibility to identify and annotate these allusions has kept alive the question as to how closely his satire relates to the society of his times (see Yates 1981; also *HKA: Stücke 18/i*: 110-15; *Stücke 19*: 117-24). Over and above reassessments of his satirical range arising directly out of work on the edition, investigations have appeared on such topics as Nestroy's unidealizing depiction of family life, his treatment of the position of women against the background of the contemporary debate on emancipation, his satire of trends within the theater of his time, and the politically "subversive" implications of his use of language (Schmidt-Dengler 1982; Yates 1985c; Münz 1988; Decker 1987). There is still a shortage of studies concentrating on the plays of the 1850s, which in Berghaus's view express an increasingly pessimistic view of society (Berghaus

1985). The closeness of his work to the realities of popular life and work in the Biedermeier period, on the other hand, is reflected in a reinterpretation of *Der böse Geist Lumpacivagabundus* as an exposé, against the background of rising alcoholism, of the materialist morality of the bourgeoisie in which the uncritically conformist Leim is integrated (Mills 1990), and has also been explored in three informative and copiously documented essays by the Viennese social historian Wolfgang Häusler (Häusler 1989, 1991, 1993). By comparison, it is disappointing that Heinz Müller-Dietz, considering the range of criminality displayed in Nestroy's work, confines himself to admiring the skill with which the motifs are explored linguistically, rather than relating them to the social background (Müller-Dietz 1979); it is a theme that would surely repay investigation by a social historian. On the other hand, it is important that Nestroy criticism should not regress into over-literalist and reductive readings of the plays as documents of various social determinants. A useful corrective has been offered by Louise Adey Huish in an elegantly written discussion of five plays from the period 1838-42 (including both *Der Talisman* and *Einen Jux will er sich machen*): she suggests that after abandoning the *Zauberstück* Nestroy may have "compensated for the eradication of the magic world as the location of fantasy by increasing the elasticity of the real world" (Adey Huish 1993: 28), and argues that the characteristic effect his comedy makes is derived from "an imagined freedom from constraints" (27), in which language and situation work together to achieve a life-affirming escape into fantasy.

In the more sensitive area where social history overlaps with politics, debate has been advanced by two particularly substantial contributions by Colin Walker, of the Queen's University of Belfast. One is a detailed exposition of the satirical treatment of the Redemptorists (*Ligorianer*) in *Freiheit in Krähwinkel* against the background of the history of the order, the hostility to it in Vienna, and its expulsion in 1848. This essay concludes with a critical reassessment of the ambivalent ending of the play, in which Walker argues that "by endorsing the expulsion ... Nestroy was undermining the message of his own play — that the Viennese were playing at revolution" (Walker 1990: 107). An earlier article, also carefully documented, sparked off an extended debate on the vexed question of anti-Semitism. We are talking here, of course, of a period before the rise of the virulent political anti-Semitism that developed in Austria in the last quarter of the nineteenth century; nevertheless, Walker reached conclusions critical of the "insensitivity" of Nestroy's comedy, arguing that "in his satirical depiction of Viennese Jews Nestroy was using themes which had been used in the political propaganda of the antisemites," and that, however unwittingly, he was "giving grist to the mill of the more zealous antisemites" (Walker 1981: 107-9). This prompted further reviews of the issue by Friedrich Walla and Jürgen Hein (Walla 1985; Hein 1988b). It is in the nature of the satirist that he is critical of social groups he treats and, in Nestroy's case, of distinctive ways of speaking; and in the main text at issue, *Judith und Holofernes*, not only are the attitudes portrayed in the Bethulia scenes (which include several close parallels with Hebbel's text) based on the fearfulness and bickering in Hebbel's Act Three and the fanaticism reported in Act Five; they also function in my view as a *positive* norm, a sample of reality, to enforce Nestroy's parodistic point. But this question of intention is still unresolved; it is complicated by shifts in perception between the mid-nineteenth century and today as well as by the element of parody in *Judith und Holofernes*, and is also related to the wider difficulty of defining the political thrust of Nestroy's plays.

The actor-dramatist is all too easily identified with his characters. Nestroy would appear on stage and deliver lines — often memorably pithy lines — which he himself had written but which, whether within the plot proper or in the solo scenes, are spoken by fictional characters; anyone seeking to extrapolate political implications enters a methodological minefield. It is too easy to say, as Mautner does in a brief essay on *Der Färber und sein Zwillingsbruder*, that in all Nestroy's plays his own part is made up partly of the role of the fictional character, partly of a role that he is merely "playing," so that we know intuitively where Nestroy himself is "speaking" (Mautner 1974a: 93). This hardly gets beyond the primitive association of dramatist and role prevalent in the early years of the twentieth century. The issue was aired in Preisner's monograph, where he argues that though the "ego" of the stage figures is not directly related to that of the dramatist, the intellectual, aesthetic, and moral sum total of a work creates a kind of artistic "super-ego" which is related to the empirical ego and private ethos of the dramatist (Preisner 1968: 144). Thus Preisner himself deduces Nestroy's attitude around 1848 from three elements in Kern in *Der alte Mann mit der jungen Frau*, his conception of revolution, his nihilism, and his humanitarianism. But the range and variety of Nestroy's roles, to which Walla rightly draws attention, speaks against the possibility of arguing in this way (Walla 1991: 248).

The problem has been re-examined by John McKenzie in a paper centering on the plays dealing with 1848 but also setting out to answer the general question whether there are "any criteria we can propose for approaching the political material in Nestroy's work" (McKenzie 1985: 123). Since political material is presented in a dramatic mode which creates an "apparently self-contained" fictive world, the relationship between comic artefact and political and social reality is complex: "A study of Nestroy's political comedies must take into account not only *what* he says about society and politics at the time of the 1848 Revolution, but *how* he presents his comments, *how* he handles the conventions of comedy" (124). It goes without saying that consideration of the "how" must include an appreciation of the effects he achieves from contrasts in linguistic registers, which depend on a facility in switching registers that is characteristic of spoken Viennese (see Scheichl 1994). In a subsequent essay McKenzie has demonstrated the subtlety and balance of the treatment of topical political material in Ultra's songs in *Freiheit in Krähwinkel*: particularly that in the final act (*SW* 5: 207-11), in which the stanzas are constructed antithetically, contrasting ideal and reality, presents the logic of international history ("d'Weltg'schicht"), and so shows up as an unrealistic pipe-dream the libertarian hope presented in the final stanza that in Austria ("Da gehn umg'kehrt die Sachen") the revolution will have a happy ending. The effect is one of "double perspective: Ultra's self-indulgent utopianism undermined by Nestroy's ironic voice." But, as McKenzie adds, "irony is accessible only to those who are willing to hear it"; the majority of the contemporary audience no doubt swallowed and approved Ultra's naive patriotism. "One can imagine how the song might have been performed on stage: Nestroy goes off after singing the first four strophes, is applauded and returns to sing the final strophe with the fictional conclusion that convention demands, the restoration of harmony" (McKenzie 1993: 177).

McKenzie's fundamental methodological point is that the quality of "deliberate contrivance" in Nestroy's farce, which combines with "his predilection for aphorism and extended metaphor" (McKenzie 1985: 126) to make it extremely hard to determine what voice is speaking at any given point within the fiction, contributes to the difficulty of pinning down the standpoint of Nestroy himself:

> What we are faced with is not simply establishing the nature of the political and social criticism in a given work but attempting to discover the author's moral standpoint, his attitude to the problems his plays depict. ... Nestroy, the unswerving sceptic, did not wear his political heart on his sleeve, nor did he betray sympathy for any particular political philosophy. Constructing a picture of his political outlook is essentially an exercise in counter-suggestibility: we have to build it up bit by bit *ex negativo*, and from the welter of satirical comments we have to try to deduce his own standpoint. ...

> Above all else, we should never assume that the opinions voiced by the characters are automatically shared by the dramatist, any more than we should confuse character, narrator, and author when dealing with a work of prose fiction. ... (McKenzie 1985: 124-26).

This is especially pertinent to the vexed question "whether Nestroy changed his political spots between 1848 and 1849": it is all too easy to fall foul of the danger of assuming that Nestroy and his central figures "are somehow identical, if not in their roles then in their function as *raisonneurs*. But Nestroy was not an Ultra or a Wendelin and he certainly was no Heugeig'n" (McKenzie 1985: 133) — a point that is made only more complex if we also take into account the element of political calculation that both McKenzie and Peter von Matt perceive in the political dicta in the post-1848 plays, in particular the controversial *Lady und Schneider* (Matt 1976: 15; McKenzie 1985: 134).

Fed by ever-growing knowledge of the dramatist's working conditions and working practices, Nestroy criticism has undoubtedly advanced in sophistication since the end of the 1970s. The drawback to this concentration on questions of practice and technique is that the new knowledge we command has not yet been reflected in a corresponding increase in large-scale critical and interpretative studies. In 1980 Peter K. Jansen lamented the shortage of interpretative studies of single Nestroy plays; eleven years later Walla repeated the point, arguing that critical interpretations of individual works are a prerequisite of serious appreciation of his dramatic work, and that there are still not enough of them (Jansen 1980: 247; Walla 1991: 242-43). Against this one might point to the short introductory appreciations of plays in the critical edition and to several essays devoted to the interpretation of single texts, in part relating Nestroy's writing to his biography and to concerns in his private life, which have arisen out of work on the edition (Walla 1979a, 1979b on *Der Tod am Hochzeitstage*; Hüttner 1980b on *Der Treulose*; Walla 1981a on *Prinz Friedrich*; Aust 1987 on *Kampl*; Hein 1988a on *Der Zerrissene*). In particular *Der Zerrissene* has been the object of much discussion, new thematic interpretations stressing the coherence of the wordplay in relation to the central motifs of friendship and sexuality (Yates 1979; Stroszeck 1988), while Cersowsky has proposed a reading of the play as playing parodistically with characteristic elements of tragic drama (Cersowsky 1992: 116-22). Nestroy's treatment of the theme of friendship has also been explored in relation to his combination of melodrama and satire in *Mein Freund* (Aust 1988).

But this is still not wholly to answer Walla's point, which is that what is needed is interpretations of individual works as artistic entities, to be taken on their own terms, rather than just as examples of general points about Nestroy. There are many essays about single plays; but they still tend to be essays about the author rather than close readings of specific texts. This is true not only of some of the older articles (e.g. Mautner 1958; Bauer 1968). To take a recent essay on *Der böse Geist Lumpacivagabundus* as just one example of many, it locates the play in the history of the genre; it outlines the genesis; it suggests the relation of the work to other Nestroy plays and to the social background; it discusses the moral and surveys the reception (Hein 1988d). In short, its basic character is introductory rather than critical. There are exceptions to this pattern; but other than the interpretations of *Der Zerrissene* mentioned above they are relatively few in number, and they center on a mere handful of the best-known plays. Typical in this respect is Cersowsky's introductory study, which concentrates on five plays, maintaining that to know a few Nestroy plays is in effect to know them all, and that there is no substantial development in his work — assumptions that are as superficial as they are unhistorical (Cersowsky 1992: 10, 151).

One of the most substantial essays on a single play is still Jansen's reading of *Der Talisman*. This play too has been the subject of several interpretative articles, which tend to concentrate on the social tensions explored in it (e.g. Klotz 1980: 45-55; Greiner 1992); Jansen goes further, showing how the radical satire depends on Nestroy's deployment of the utopian structure of a *Märchen*-like plot (Jansen 1980). The theme of utopianism, in this case in Nestroy's satiric language, is also pursued by Anthony S. Coulson, who defines the characteristic satiric ambiguity created by the role-consciousness of Nestroy's figures and explores it in lengthy analyses of individual texts, the weight falling mainly on *Der Talisman, Einen Jux will er sich machen*, and *Der Zerrissene* (Coulson 1987). More recently still, Hauke Stroszeck has published an ingenious interpretation of *Der Talisman* as centering on a figure comparable with the prodigal son and as elaborating the idea that the last shall be first (Stroszeck 1990: 22). In his view Nestroy's plays draw their fundamental impulse from the "negative reflection" of Christian motifs (55). Reversal of religious and biblical elements is certainly characteristic of Nestroy (as, for example, in *Der Zauberer Sulphur...*, a parodistic variation on a Raupach original). Stroszeck's book was dismissed by Hillach as no better than hermeneutic sleight of hand (Hillach 1991), and it may be true that individual points are unconvincing — e.g. the attempt to read soteriological overtones into the prediction of a "fortunate catastrophe" ("eine günstige Katastrophe" [*HKA: Stücke 17/i*: 21]), where an allusion to the conventional happy ending of comedy, of a kind typical of Nestroy, is much more obvious (Stroszeck 1990: 43). As Frau von Cypressenburg perceives, Titus is a figure who "lavishes twenty lofty words on what can be said in a single syllable" ("Wie verschwenderisch er mit 20 erhabenen Worten das sagt was man mit einer Sylbe sagen kann!" [*Stücke 17/i*: 50]); it is typical of him that he finds a consciously literary euphemism for what Gottlieb Herb, the Nestroy role in *Der Schützling*, simply calls "ein fröhliches Ende" (*SW* 7: 238). Similarly it is not self-evident that allusions to salvationism or even biblical allusions predominate in Titus's literary word-spinning (Stroszeck 1990: 64); certainly in the salon scene in the third act the allusions are specifically to the genres of the dialect theater. Nevertheless, the book contains many suggestive insights, and Stroszeck's claim that the cumulative argumentative force of the resonances in Nestroy's dialogue has escaped previous scholarship (55) deserves to be taken seriously: the attempt to draw together the resonances of Nestroy's wordplay ("Wortkombinatorik" [12]), to show the extent to which he builds up an associative network of images, is challenging and stimulating.

Simultaneously with these stirrings of serious interpretative criticism, Nestroy has begun to be better known internationally outside academic circles, with an increased number of translations available. These are not wholly successful: the range of effects he achieves from subtle gradations of Viennese dialect (see Scheichl 1994), and his dependence for satirical and parodistic effects on contrasts between dialect and stagy literary German, mean that "most of Nestroy's dialogue is untranslatable" (Esslin 1962: 241). This has been challenged as a matter of principle (Yates 1982); but anyone who has tried his or her hand at it knows that the interplay of registers dependent on a specific dialect presents immense problems. The most recent critical account of the translations so far available in English rightly ends with an encouragement to other translators to try their hand; but this is tempered by a realistic recognition of the difficulties faced by the translator "as soon as Nestroy's language becomes more complex and vocabulary tinged with dialect has to be rendered" (Grimstad 1990: 446). Joseph Fabry, a Viennese émigré, has recounted how when first he went to the USA he realized that he would never be able to speak English without an accent but that he could write it without an accent. In fact, however, the translations he published in collaboration with a fellow-émigré, Max Knight (1967), have a strongly American flavor, and the "accent" cannot but be unfaithful. The most successful Nestroy version in the theater is Tom Stoppard's *On the Razzle*, a very free adaptation of *Einen Jux will er sich machen*, which was first published in 1981 and was reprinted "with corrections" — that is, reflecting the changes made to the text for performance — the following year. The market is still wide open for translations less free than Stoppard's adaptation but with equal linguistic verve, and it is recognized that there is an urgent need for new translators to take on this challenging task (Grimstad 1990: 447; Yates 1993a: 166).

Because reliable scholarship on Nestroy has been late to develop and has developed unevenly, there are also exciting openings for further original criticism. The state of Nestroy studies at the beginning of the 1990s has been addressed in three surveys (Hein 1990; Walla 1991; Yates 1993a). The longest of these, Jürgen Hein's volume in the Sammlung Metzler series, offers an account of the resources on which scholarship depends and a survey of research on Nestroy's life and career, his relation to the theater, his dramatic writing, and the reception of his work. All surveys of criticism are out-of-date as soon as they appear; but Hein's is nevertheless an invaluable summary, which includes some masterly condensing of complex issues, such as a tabular résumé of attempts to divide Nestroy's work into periods (64-65) and a summary of Nestroy's working methods (103-04). It is also a treasure trove of topics needing further investigation. Hein, a professor at the University of Münster, is Vice-President of the International Nestroy Society and the most prolific editor of the new edition (*HKA*). He has also been a central pillar of the annual conferences that have been taking place at Schwechat since 1975, and he has earned the gratitude of Nestroy scholars with his series of *Forschungsberichte*, of which the 1990 volume is the culmination; not the least of their merits is the generosity with which he has pointed out areas of investigation that still need to be addressed.

A major new critical study, updating Mautner's perceptions in the light of new documentation, is still far off. There will never be a definitive study; one of the lessons to be drawn from the history of reception is that critical and even biographical studies are always superseded, as perspectives, expectations, and critical fashions change. But if one recalls that Hannemann, writing just before the new edition was launched, lamented that the lack of a reliable text, together with lack of autobiographical records, amounted to a "hermeneutic handicap of the first order" (Hannemann 1977: 2), it is clear that the re-editing of the texts and the documentation provided in the new edition (backed up by the journal *Nestroyana*) are correcting that deficiency and providing the soundest basis possible for critical scholarship.

It is, I think, a particularly healthy sign that a lot of the work on the edition is being undertaken by scholars who are not Viennese. Nestroy's work is of course deeply rooted in Vienna, but no service is done it by pretending that it is insuperably local, condemning it to a perpetual provincial marginality. The considerations involved are those implicit in Kraus's designation of Nestroy as not merely an Austrian dialect dramatist but a German satirist ("kein österreichischer Dialektdichter, sondern ein deutscher Satiriker" [Kraus 1925: 25]). The theatrical literature of the western world is not so overstocked with comic dramatists of the first rank that it can afford to remain ignorant of a satirist of Nestroy's stature. But the battle for the recognition of that stature has still not been won: the challenge for critics of tomorrow is clear.

Bibliography

Nestroy's Works

The list includes all Nestroy's plays and adaptations of which texts are extant. The date given is that of composition and/or first performance. Publication details of those plays printed during Nestroy's lifetime and other first editions are added under the title concerned; also a reference to the new standard edition (*HKA*) where appropriate. The abbreviation "m. G." denotes "mit Gesang"; "P. m. G." denotes "Posse mit Gesang." The figure in brackets after the genre gives the number of acts. The principal Viennese theaters are abbreviated as follows: ThW (Theater an der Wien); LTh (Theater in der Leopoldstadt); CTh (Carltheater).

c. 1827 *Prinz Friedrich* [*von Corsica*]. Historisch-romantisches Drama (5). Music: Adolf Müller. Première: ThW 1841. First edition in book form under the title *Rudolf Prinz von Korsika*, ed. Gustav Pichler, Vienna: Heidrich 1947. (*HKA*: *Stücke 1*: 3-88.)

1827 *Zwölf Mädchen in Uniform.* Posse (1), after Louis Angely. Première: Ständisches Theater (Schauspielhaus), Graz, 1827. First published, ed. Gustav Pichler, Vienna: Luckmann-Verlag n.d. [1943].

1827 *Der Zettelträger Papp.* Vorspiel (1). Music: Franz Volkert. Première: Ständisches Theater (Schauspielhaus), Graz, 1827. Published in *Zwei unbekannte Stücke Johann Nestroy's*, ed. Fritz Brukner. Vienna: Knepler 1910: 17-34. (*HKA*: *Stücke 1*: 91-106.)

1828 *Dreißig Jahre aus dem Leben eines Lumpen.* Zauberspiel m. G. und Tanz (2). Première: Ständisches Theater (Schauspielhaus), Graz, 1828 under the title *Des Wüstlings Radikalkur oder Die dreißig Jahre der Verbannung.* Published 1979, *HKA*: *Stücke 1*: 109-78.

1829 *Der Tod am Hochzeitstage oder Mann, Frau, Kind.* Zauberspiel (2). Music: Franz Roser. Première: Theater in der Josefstadt 1829. Published 1924, *SW* 1:87-217. (*HKA*: *Stücke 1*: 243-343.)

1832 *Der gefühlvolle Kerkermeister oder Adelheid, die verfolgte Witib.* Parodie (3). Music: Adolf Müller. Première: ThW 1832. Published 1891, *CG* 10: 1-44.

1832 *Nagerl und Handschuh oder Die Schicksale der Familie Maxenpfutsch.* Parodie (3). Music: Adolf Müller. Première: ThW 1832. Published 1891, *CG* 10: 91-134.

1832 *Die Verbannung aus dem Zauberreiche.* Zauberspiel m. G. (2). Music: Franz Roser and Adolf Müller. Première: ThW 1832. Published 1891, *CG* 10: 45-90. (*HKA: Stücke 1*: 181-237.)

1832 *Der Theaterdiener, die Benefizvorstellung und das Quodlibet.* Vorspiel (1). Première: ThW 1832. Published 1927, *SW* 9: 449-57.

1832 *Zampa der Tagdieb oder Die Braut von Gips.* Parodie (3). Music: Adolf Müller. Première: ThW 1832. Published 1891, *CG* 9: 65-114.

1832 *Der konfuse Zauberer oder Treue und Flatterhaftigkeit.* Original-Zauberspiel (3). Music: Adolf Müller. Première: ThW 1832. Published 1891, *CG* 10: 135-82.

1832 *Die Zauberreise in die Ritterzeit oder Die Übermütigen.* Original-Zauberposse (Vorspiel + 3). Music: Adolf Müller. Première: ThW 1832. Published 1891, *CG* 11: 1-45.

1832 *Genius, Schuster und Marqueur oder Die Pyramiden der Verzauberung.* Zauberposse (3). Not performed in Nestroy's lifetime. Published 1924, *SW* 1: 419-527.

1833 *Der Feenball oder Tischler, Schneider und Schlosser.* Faschingsposse (3). Not performed in Nestroy's lifetime. Published 1924, *SW* 1: 529-602. (*HKA: Stücke 5*: 3-64.)

1833 *Der böse Geist Lumpacivagabundus oder Das liederliche Kleeblatt.* Zauberposse m. G. (3). Music: Adolf Müller. Première: ThW 1833. Published Vienna: Wallishausser, 1835. (*HKA: Stücke 5*: 69-132.)

1833 *Robert der Teuxel.* Parodierende Zauberposse (3). Music: Adolf Müller. Première: ThW 1833. Published 1891, *CG* 9: 115-151. (*HKA: Stücke 6*: 75-148.)

1833 *Der Tritschtratsch.* Locale P. m. G. (1). Music: Adolf Müller. Première: ThW 1833. Published 1891, *CG* 7: 1-29. (*HKA: Stücke 7/2*: 5-42.)

1833 *Das Verlobungsfest im Feenreiche oder Die Gleichheit der Jahre.* Zauberposse (3). Not performed in Nestroy's lifetime. Published 1924, *SW* 2: 379-456. (*HKA: Stücke 7/1*: 5-65.)

1834 *Der Zauberer Suphurelektrimagneticophosphoratus und die Fee Walpurgiblocksbergiseptemtrionalis oder Die Abenteuer in der Sklaverei.* Zauberposse m. G. (3). Music: Adolf Müller. Première: ThW 1834. Published 1891, *CG* 11: 47-90. (*HKA: Stücke 6*: 5-70.)

1834 *Müller, Kohlenbrenner und Sesseltrager oder Die Träume von Schale und Kern.* Zauberspiel (3). Music: Adolf Müller. Première: ThW 1834. Published 1891, *CG* 8: 117-67. (*HKA: Stücke 7/2*: 47-127.)

1833 *Die Gleichheit der Jahre.* Local-Posse (4). Music: Adolf Müller. Première: ThW 1834. Published 1890, *CG* 3: 155-204. (*HKA: Stücke 7/1*: 71-140.)

1834 *Die Familien Zwirn, Knieriem und Leim oder Der Welt-Untergangs-Tag.* Zauberspiel (2). Music: Adolf Müller. Première: ThW 1834. Published 1890, *CG* 1: 109-56.

1834 *Die Fahrt mit dem Dampfwagen.* Vorspiel (1). Première: ThW 1834. Published 1891, *CG* 7: 31-43.

1835 *Weder Lorbeerbaum noch Bettelstab.* Parodierende Posse (3). Music: Adolf Müller. Première: ThW 1835. Published 1891, *CG* 9: 153-95.

1835 *Eulenspiegel, oder: Schabernack über Schabernack.* P. m. G. (4). Music: Adolf Muller. Première: ThW 1835. Published Vienna: Wallishausser 1839.

1835 *Zu ebener Erde und erster Stock oder Die Launen des Glückes.* Lokalposse m. G. (3). Music: Adolf Müller. Première: ThW 1835. Published Vienna: Wallishausser 1838.

1836 *Der Treulose oder Saat und Ernte.* Dramatisches Gemälde (2). Music: Adolf Müller. Première: ThW 1836. Published 1891, *CG* 5: 1-74.

1836 *Die beiden Nachtwandler oder Das Notwendige und das Überflüssige.* P. m. G. (2). Music: Adolf Müller. Première: ThW 1836. Published 1891, *CG* 7: 149-94.

1836 *Der Affe und der Bräutigam.* P. m. G. (3). Music: Georg Ott. Première: ThW 1836. Published 1891, *CG* 5: 75-121.

1837 *Eine Wohnung ist zu vermieten in der Stadt, eine Wohnung ist zu verlassen in der Vorstadt, eine Wohnung mit Garten ist zu haben in Hietzing.* Lokal-P. m. G. (3). Music: Adolf Müller. Première: ThW 1837. Published 1891, *CG* 8: 169-222. (*HKA: Stücke 12*: 5-82.)

1837 *Moppels Abenteuer im Viertel unter Wiener Wald, in Neu-Seeland und Marokko.* P. (2). Music: Adolf Müller. Première: ThW 1837. Published in *Zwei unbekannte Stücke Johann Nestroy's,* ed. Fritz Brukner. Vienna: Knepler 1910: 35-96. (*HKA: Stücke 12*: 85-135.)

1837 *Das Haus der Temperamente.* P. (2). Music: Adolf Müller. Première: ThW 1837. Published 1891, *CG* 11: 171-258. (*HKA: Stücke 13*: 5-191.)

1838 *Glück, Mißbrauch und Rückkehr oder Das Geheimnis des grauen Hauses.* P. m. G. (5). Music: Adolf Müller. Première: ThW 1838. Published Vienna: Wallishausser 1845. (*HKA: Stücke 14*: 5-89.)

1838 *Der Kobold, oder Staberl im Feendienst.* Parodierende Zauberposse m. G. (4). Music: Adolf Müller. Première: ThW 1838. Published 1891, *CG* 10: 183-221. (*HKA: Stücke 14*: 95-150.)

1838 *Gegen Torheit gibt es kein Mittel.* Lustiges Trauerspiel m. G. (3). Music: Adolf Müller. Première: ThW 1838. Published 1891, *CG* 8: 57-116.

1839 *Die verhängnisvolle Faschings-Nacht.* P. m. G. (3). Music: Adolf Müller. Première: ThW 1839. Published Vienna: Wallishausser 1841.

1840 *Der Färber und sein Zwillingsbruder.* P. m. G. (3). Music: Adolf Müller. Première: ThW 1840. Published 1890, *CG* 3: 205-57.

1840 *Der Erbschleicher.* P. m. G. (4). Music: Adolf Müller. Première: ThW 1840. Published 1891, *CG* 7: 93-147.

1840 *Die zusammengestoppelte Komödie.* Vorspiel (1). Première: ThW 1840.

1840 *Der Talisman.* P. m. G. (3). Music: Adolf Müller. Première: WTh 1840. Published Vienna: Wallishausser 1843. (*HKA: Stücke 17/i*: 5-86.)

1841 *Das Mädl aus der Vorstadt, oder Ehrlich währt am längsten.* Posse (3). Music: Adolf Müller. Première: ThW 1841. Published Vienna: Wallishausser 1845.

1842 *Einen Jux will er sich machen.* P. m. G. (3). Music: Adolf Müller. Première: ThW 1842. Published Vienna: Wallishausser 1844. (*HKA: Stücke 18/1*: 9-95.)

1842 *Die Papiere des Teufels oder Der Zufall.* P. m. G. (Vorspiel + 3). Music: Adolf Müller. Première: ThW 1842. Published 1890, *CG* 2: 1-64.

1843 *Liebesgeschichten und Heiratssachen.* P. m. G. (3). Music: Michael Hebenstreit. Première: ThW 1843. Published 1891, *CG* 7: 245-98. (*HKA: Stücke 19*: 5-84.)

1843 *Die dramatischen Zimmerherrn.* Vorspiel (1). Première: ThW 1843. Published 1927, *SW* 9: 458-68. (*HKA: Stücke 19*: 88-97.)

1843 *Nur Ruhe!.* P. m. G. (3) Music: Adolf Müller. Première: ThW 1843. Published 1891, *CG* 12: 33-89. (*HKA: Stücke 20*: 5-85.)

1844 *Eisenbahnheiraten oder Wien, Neustadt, Brünn.* P. m. G. (3). Music: Andreas Scutta. Première: ThW 1844. Published 1891, *CG* 7: 45-92. (*HKA: Stücke 20*: 91-160.)

1844 *Hinüber — Herüber — Hinüber — Herüber.* Intermezzo (1). Première: ThW 1844. Published Berlin: Kolbe 1852. (*HKA: Stücke 21*: 3-20.)

1844 *Der Zerrissene.* P. m. G. (3). Music: Adolf Müller. Première: ThW 1844. Published Vienna: Wallishausser 1845. (*HKA: Stücke 21*: 25-93.)

1845 *Die beiden Herrn Söhne.* P. m. G. (4). Music: Adolf Müller. Première: ThW 1845. Published 1891, *CG* 8: 1-56.

1845 *Das Gewürzkrämer-Kleeblatt.* P. m. G. (3). Music: Adolf Müller. Première: ThW 1845. Published 1891, *CG* 7: 195-244.

1845 *Unverhofft*. P. m. G. (3). Music: Adolf Müller. Première: ThW 1845. Published Vienna: Wallishausser 1848.

1846 *Der Unbedeutende* P. m. G. (3). Music: Adolf Müller. Première: LTh 1846. Published Vienna: Wallishausser 1849.

1846 *Zwei ewige Juden für einen* [*Der fliegende Holländer zu Fuße*]. Burleske m. G. (2). Music: Adolf Müller. Première: LTh 1846. Published 1891, *CG* 5: 123-72.

1847 *Der Schützling*. P. m. G. (4). Music: Adolf Müller. Première: LTh 1847. Published 1891, *CG* 6: 65-132.

1847 *Die schlimmen Buben in der Schule*. Burleske m. G. (1). Music: Michael Hebenstreit. Première: CTh 1847. Published 1890, *CG* 1: 221-50.

1848 *Martha oder Die Mischmonder Markt-Mägde-Mietung*. Parodierende P. m. G. (3). Music: Michael Hebenstreit. Première: CTh 1848. Published 1891, *CG* 9: 197-236.

1848 *Die Anverwandten*. P. m. G. (5). Music: Michael Hebenstreit. Première: CTh 1848. Published 1890, *CG* 4: 227-83.

1848 *Freiheit in Krähwinkel*. P. m. G. (3). Music: Michael Hebenstreit. Première: CTh 1848. Published Vienna: Wallishausser 1849.

1849 *Lady und Schneider*. P. m. G. (2). Music: Michael Hebenstreit. Première: CTh 1849. Published 1891, *CG* 6: 201-54.

1849 *Judith und Holofernes*. Travestie (1). Music: Michael Hebenstreit. Première: CTh 1849. Published 1891, *CG* 9: 237-59.

1849 *Höllenangst*. P. m. G. (3). Music: Michael Hebenstreit. Première: CTh 1849. Published 1890, *CG* 3: 55-106.

1849 *Der alte Mann mit der jungen Frau*. P. m. G. (4). [Not performed in Nestroy's lifetime; first performance in an adaptation under the title *Der Flüchtling*, Deutsches Volkstheater, 1890]. Published 1891, *CG* 11: 113-69.

1850 *"Sie sollen ihn nicht haben" oder Der holländische Bauer*. P. m. G. (3). Music: Michael Hebenstreit. Première: CTh 1850. Published 1891, *CG* 6: 149-99.

1850 *Karikaturen-Charivari mit Heiratszweck*. P. m. G. (3). Music: Michael Hebenstreit. Première: CTh 1850. Published 1891, *CG* 5: 173-222.

1850 *Alles will den Propheten sehen*. P. m. G. (3). Music: Carl Franz Stenzel. Première: CTh 1850. Published 1891, *CG* 6: 255-306.

1850 *Verwickelte Geschichte*. P. m. G. (2). Music: Carl Franz Stenzel. Première: CTh 1850. Published 1890, *CG* 2: 125-54.

1851 *Mein Freund*. P. m. G. (Vorspiel + 3). Music: Carl Franz Stenzel. Première: CTh 1851. Published Vienna: Wallishausser n.d.; Lell [*ca.* 1851].

1851 *Der gutmütige [gemütliche] Teufel oder Die Geschichte vom Bauer und von der Bäuerin.* Zauberspiel m. G. (1). Music: Carl Binder. Première: CTh 1851. Published 1891, *CG* 9: 261-87.

1852 *Kampl, oder: Das Mädchen mit Millionen und die Nähterin.* P. m. G. (3). Music: Carl Binder. Première: CTh 1852. Published Vienna: Prix [1852]. (*HKA: Stücke 31*: 1-133.)

1853 *Heimliches Geld, heimliche Liebe.* P. m. G. (3). Music: Carl Binder. Première: CTh 1853. Published 1891, *CG* 6: 1-64. *(HKA: Stücke 32*: 5-102.)

1854 *Theaterg'schichten durch Liebe, Intrige, Geld und Dummheit.* P. m. G. (2). Music: Carl Binder. Première: CTh 1854. Published Vienna: Klopf und Eurich [1854]. (*HKA: Stücke 33*: 5-81.)

1855. *"Nur keck!".* P. m. G. (3). Not performed in Nestroy's lifetime. [Première: Wiener Bürgertheater, 1943.] Published: *Neue Freie Presse,* 1921. First edition in book form, ed. Peter Sturmbusch, Vienna: Interterritorialer Verlag "Renaissance." [1922]. (*HKA: Stücke 34*: 5-111.)

1857 *Umsonst!* P. m. G. und Tanz. (3) Music: Carl Binder. Première: CTh 1857. Published 1891, *CG* 5: 223-99.

1857 *Tannhäuser.* Zukunftsposse mit vergangener Musik und gegenwärtigen Gruppierungen (3). Music: Carl Binder. Première: CTh 1857. Published Vienna: Wallishausser 1857.

c. 1858 *Zeitvertreib.* P. (1). Not performed in Nestroy's lifetime. Published 1891, *CG* 12: 1-32.

1858 *Ein gebildeter Hausknecht.* Posse (1) after David Kalisch. Première: CTh 1858. Published, ed. Gustav Pichler, Vienna: Luckmann-Verlag n.d. [1943].

1859 *Lohengrin.* Musikalisch-dramatische Parodie (4). Music: Carl Binder. Première: CTh 1859. Published 1891, *CG* 11: 91-112.

1862 *Frühere Verhältnisse* P. m. G. (1). Music: Anton Maria Storch. Première: Kai-Theater 1862. Published 1891, *CG* 8: 223-46.

1862 *Häuptling Abendwind oder Das greuliche Festmahl.* Operette [Indianische Faschingsburleske] (1). Music: Jacques Offenbach. Première: Kai-Theater 1862. Published, ed. Karl Glossy, *Neue Freie Presse,* 26 May 1912 (no. 17154): 95-102 and 2 June 1912 (no. 17160): 32-35.

Editions

1873. *Aus Nestroy. Eine kleine Erinnerungsgabe. Mit einem biographischen Vorworte,* ed. Leopold Rosner. Vienna: L. Rosner.

1890-91. *Gesammelte Werke,* ed. Vincenz Chiavacci and Ludwig Ganghofer. 12 vols. Stuttgart: Bonz. (Abbreviated: *CG.*)

[1908]. *Nestroys Werke. Auswahl in zwei Teilen*, ed. Otto Rommel. Bongs Goldene Klassiker-Bibliothek. Berlin, Leipzig, Wien, Stuttgart: Bong.

1910. *Zwei unbekannte Stücke Johann Nestroy's*, ed. Fritz Brukner. Vienna: Knepler.

[1911]. *Johann Nestroys ausgewählte Werke. Vier Teile in einem Band*, ed. Fritz Brukner. Leipzig: Hesse & Becker.

1924-30. *Sämtliche Werke*, ed. Fritz Brukner and Otto Rommel. 15 vols. Vienna: Schroll. (Abbreviated: *SW*.)

[1937]. *Ausgewählte Werke*, ed. Franz H. Mautner. Vienna: Otto Lorenz.

1938. *Johann Nestroys gesammelte Briefe (1831-1862). Nestroy und seine Bühne im Jahre 1848*, ed. Fritz Brukner. Vienna: Wallishausser.

1948-49. *Gesammelte Werke*, ed. Otto Rommel. 6 vols. Vienna: Schroll. (Abbreviated: *GW*.)

1955. "Unbekannte Couplets von Johann Nestroy," ed. Otto Rommel. *Jahrbuch der Gesellschaft für Wiener Theaterforschung 1951/1952*: 132-46.

1966. *Nestroys Werke in zwei Bänden*, ed. Paul Reimann, with notes by Hans Böhm. 2 vols. Bibliothek deutscher Klassiker. 2nd edition. Berlin and Weimar: Aufbau.

1970. *Komödien*, ed. Franz H. Mautner. 3 vols. Frankfurt a. M.: Insel.

1977- . *Sämtliche Werke. Historisch-kritische Ausgabe*, ed. Jürgen Hein and Johann Hüttner [from 1992: Jürgen Hein, Johann Hüttner, Walter Obermaier, and W. Edgar Yates]. Vienna, Munich: Jugend und Volk. (Abbreviated: *HKA*.)

Includes:

1977. *Briefe*, ed. Walter Obermaier.

1977. *Johann Nestroy im Bild. Eine Ikonographie*, compiled by Heinrich Schwarz, ed. Johann Hüttner and Otto G. Schindler.

1979- . *Stücke*. (The following volumes had appeared by the end of 1993: 1, 5, 6, 7/I, 7/II (ed. Friedrich Walla), 12, 13, 14 (ed. W. E. Yates), 17/I (ed. Jürgen Hein and Peter Haida), 18/I (ed. W. E. Yates), 19, 20, 21 (ed. Jürgen Hein), 31 (ed. Hugo Aust), 32, 33 (ed. Jürgen Hein), and 34 (ed. W. E. Yates).

Selected Translations and Adaptations

Mélesville and Carmouche. 1842. *Du haut en bas ou Banquier et fripiers*. Comédie-vaudeville en deux actes. Reprinted in Stieg and Valentin 1991. 195-296. [French adaptation of *Zu ebener Erde und erster Stock*.]

Kraus, Karl. 1920. *Das Notwendige und das Überflüssige. (Nach "Die beiden Nachtwandler")*. Posse mit Gesang in zwei Akten von Johann Nestroy. Bearbeitet von Karl Kraus. Vienna: Lányi.

Kraus, Karl. 1925. *Der konfuse Zauberer oder Treue und Flatterhaftigkeit.* Zauberspiel in vier Akten von Johann Nestroy. Bearbeitet von Karl Kraus nach *Der konfuse Zauberer* und *Der Tod am Hochzeitstage.* Vienna, Leipzig: Lányi.

Wilder, Thornton. 1955. *The Matchmaker.* A Farce. Reprinted in Wilder, *Our Town, The Skin of Our Teeth, The Matchmaker.* Penguin Plays. Harmondsworth 1962. 179-281. [Based on *Einen Jux will er sich machen.*]

1960-61. "Liberty Comes to Krähwinkel." Adapted and translated by Sybil and Colin Welch. *Tulane Drama Review* 5, no. 4: 135-74. [Translation of *Freiheit in Krähwinkel.*]

1967. *Three Comedies by Johann Nestroy. A Man Full of Nothing, The Talisman, Love Affairs and Wedding Bells.* Translated (and fondly tampered with) by Max Knight and Joseph Fabry. New York: Ungar. [Versions of *Der Zerrissene* (29-93), *Der Talisman* (95-174), and *Liebesgeschichten und Heiratssachen* (175-258).]

1974. *Teatro.* A cura di Italo Alighiero Chiusano. Milan: Adelphi. [Italian versions of *Lumpacivagabundus* (9-71, by Ervino Pocar), *Zu ebener Erde und erster Stock* (73-249), *Einen Jux will er sich machen* (251-348), *Der Zerrissene* (349-424), *Freiheit in Krähwinkel* (425-98), and *Judith und Holofernes* (499-537).]

Stoppard, Tom. 1981. *On the Razzle. Adapted from "Einen Jux will er sich machen" by Johann Nestroy.* London, Boston: Faber and Faber. Reprinted with corrections 1982.

1983. *Színművek.* Budapest: Európa Könyvkiadó. [Hungarian versions of *Lumpacivagabundus* (5-69, by Dezsö Tandori), *Die beiden Nachtwandler* (71-141, by István Eörsi), *Der Talisman* (143-220, by Dezsö Mészöly), *Der Zerrissene* (221-91, by Gábor Hajnal), *Freiheit in Krähwinkel* (293-362, by József Viola), and *Der alte Mann mit der jungen Frau* (363-439, by Gábor Görgey).]

1985. *"L'Homme déchiré"* (Texte français: Jean-Louis Besson et Heinz Schwarzinger) *suivi de "Une Pinte de bon sang aux dépens d'autrui"* (Texte français: Félix Kreissler). Rouen: Publications de l'Université de Rouen. [French versions of *Der Zerrissene* and *Einen Jux will er sich machen.*]

1986. *Three Viennese Comedies by Johann Nepomuk Nestroy.* Translated by Robert Harrison and Katharina Wilson. Columbia, South Carolina: Camden House. [American translations of *Der Talisman* (15-92), *Judith und Holofernes* (93-121), and *Das Haus der Temperamente* (123-262).]

Critical Writings, cited in chronological order

Weidmann, F[ranz] C[arl]. 1834. [Review of *Die Familien Zwirn, Krieriem und Leim*]. *Theaterzeitung*, 8 November 1834 (no. 223): 893.

Saphir, M. G. 1835. [Review of *Zu ebener Erde und erster Stock*]. *Theaterzeitung*, 30 September 1835 (no. 195): 778-79.

Seidlitz, Julius [= Itzig Jeitteles]. 1837. *Die Poesie und die Poeten in Österreich im Jahre 1836*. 2 vols. Grimma: J. M. Gebhardt.

Kaiser, Friedrich. 1837. [Review of *Eine Wohnung ist zu vermieten*]. *Der Sammler*, 7 February 1837 (no. 16): 64. (Reprinted *HKA: Stücke 12*, 156-57.)

Wiest, [Franz]. 1837. [Review of *Moppels Abenteuer*]. *Theaterzeitung*, 8 May 1837 (no. 91): 365-66. (Reprinted *HKA: Stücke 12*, 182-86.)

Costenoble, Carl Ludwig. 1837. Diary entry, 2 June 1837. In Carl Ludwig Costenoble, *Aus dem Burgtheater. 1818-1837. Tagebuchblätter* [ed. Karl Glossy and Jakob Zeidler]. 2 vols. Vienna: Konegen. 1889. 2: 335-36.

Dingelstedt, Franz von. 1837. "Die Poesie in Oesterreich. 2. Dramatisches und Dramaturgik." *Beurmann's Telegraph* [= *Frankfurter Telegraph*]. 4th Quarter, nos 22-26: 169-72, 179-81, 189-91, 198-200, 205-8.

ch l——. 1837. [Review of *Das Haus der Temperamente*]. *Der Humorist*, 20 November (no. 171): 683-84. (Reprinted *HKA: Stücke 13*, 203-7.)

Tuvora, [Josef]. [Review of *Glück, Mißbrauch und Rückkehr*]. *Der Sammler*, 17 March 1838 (no. 33): 132. (Reprinted *HKA: Stücke 14*: 179-81.)

[Gross-Hoffinger, A. J.]. 1838. [Review of *Glück, Mißbrauch und Rückkehr*] (signed 'G.'). *Der Adler*, 19 March 1838 (no. 55): 244. (Reprinted *HKA: Stücke 14*: 181-82.)

Schmidt, Max. 1838. [Review of *Glück, Mißbrauch und Rückkehr*]. *Oesterreichiches Morgenblatt*, 19 March 1838 (no. 34): 136. (Reprinted *HKA: Stücke 14*: 181.)

Saphir, M. G. 1839. "Nestroy und die Wiener Lokalposse. (In Beziehung auf das neue Nestroy'sche Stück *Die verhängnißvolle Faschingsnacht*. Lokalposse in drei Aufzügen)." *Der Humorist*, 17-18 April (nos. 76-77): 303-4, 306-7. (Reprinted in Saphir, *Ausgewählte Schriften*. Brünn, Vienna: Fr. Karafiat. 1871-74. 1st Series. 6: 188-98.)

Anon. 1839. "Korrespondenz-Nachrichten" [Report on *Die verhängnisvolle Faschingsnacht*]. *Morgenblatt für gebildete Leser*, 21 May 1839 (no. 121): 484.

[Gutzkow, Karl.] 1841. [Review of *Glück, Mißbrauch und Rückkehr* and *Der Talisman*]. *Telegraph für Deutschland*. July (no. 113): 448. (Reprinted *HKA: Stücke 14*: 184; *Stücke 17/1*: 145-46.)

Naske, A. C. 1841. [Review of *Das Mädl aus der Vorstadt*]. *Der Wanderer*, 26 November 1841 (no. 282): 1135-36.

Viola, L. 1841. [Review of *Das Mädl aus der Vorstadt*]. *Wiener Zuschauer*, 1 December 1841 (no. 144): 1440-41.

Frankl, Ludwig August. 1842. "Nekrolog der Wiener Volksmuse." *Sonntags-Blätter für heimathliche Interessen*, 23 January 1842 (no. 4): 57-59.

Saphir, [M. G.]. 1842. [Review of *Einen Jux will er sich machen*]. *Der Humorist*, 12 March 1842 (no. 51): 206-7. (Reprinted *HKA: Stücke 18/1*: 125-27).

——e. 1842. [Review of *Einen Jux will er sich machen*]. *Der Adler*, 12 March 1842 (no. 61), p. 251. (Reprinted *HKA: Stücke 18/1*, 128-29.)

[Straube, Emanuel]. 1842. [Review of *Einen Jux will er sich machen*] (signed "Stbe."). *Wiener Zeitschrift für Kunst, Literatur, Theater und Mode*, 14 March 1842 (no. 52): 415-16. (Reprinted *HKA: Stücke 18/1*: 131-33.)

Lewinsky, Ignaz. 1842. [Review of *Einen Jux will er sich machen*]. *Allgemeine Wiener Musik-Zeitung*, 15 March 1842 (no. 32): 130. (Reprinted *HKA: Stücke 18/1*: 132-33).

Dingelstedt, Franz. 1842. "Eine diabolische Theaterkritik." *Wiener Zeitschrift für Kunst, Literatur, Theater und Mode*, 12 November 1842 (no. 226): 1804-07; 14 November 1842 (no. 227): 1814-15; 15 November 1842 (no. 228): 1820-22.

Wagner, Dr. 1843a. [Review of *Liebesgeschichten und Heiratssachen*]. *Sonntags-Blätter*, 26 March 1843 (no. 13): 301-2 (Reprinted *HKA: Stücke 19*: 149-50).

Nordmann, [Johannes]. 1843. [Review of *Liebesgeschichten und Heiratssachen*]. *Oesterreichisches Morgenblatt*, 29 March 1843 (no. 38): 150-51 (Reprinted *HKA: Stücke 19*: 158-60.)

Wagner, Dr. 1843b. "Die Lokalposse jüngerer Zeit." *Sonntags-Blätter*, 12 November 1843 (no. 46): 1093-95. (Reprinted *HKA: Stücke 20*: 167-70.)

Saphir, M. G. 1843. "Didaskalien." *Der Humorist*, 20 November 1843 (no. 231): 929-32.

Schindler, F[ranz] V. 1843. [Review of *Nur Ruhe!*]. *Oesterreichisches Morgenblatt*, 20 November 1843 (no. 231): 555. (Reprinted *HKA: Stücke 20*: 176-78.)

[Tuvora, Joseph]. 1844. *Briefe aus Wien. Von einem Eingebornen*. 2 vols. Hamburg: Hoffmann und Campe. 2: 72-73.

Anon. 1844a. "Korrespondenz-Nachrichten" [Report on première of *Nur Ruhe!*]. *Morgenblatt für gebildete Leser*, 3 January 1844 (no. 3): 12.

Schindler, [Franz] V. 1844. [Review of *Eisenbahnheiraten*]. *Oesterreichisches Morgenblatt*, 5 January 1844 (no. 3): 10-11. (Reprinted *HKA: Stücke 20*: 265-68.)

Anon. 1844b. "Korrespondenz-Nachrichten" [Report on première of *Eisenbahnheirathen*]. *Morgenblatt für gebildete Leser*, 10 April 1844 (no. 87): 348.

Anon. 1844c. "Korrespondenz-Nachrichten" [Report on première of *Der Zerrissene*]. *Morgenblatt für gebildete Leser*, 6 June 1844 (no. 136): 544. (Reprinted in Yates 1992: 86.)

Gutzkow, Karl. 1845. "Wiener Eindrücke." In Gutzkow, *Gesammelte Werke. Vollständig umgearbeitete Ausgabe*. 12 vols. Frankfurt a.M.: Literarische Anstalt (J. Rütten). 1845-46. 3: 269-335.

Markbreiter, M. 1845. [Review of *Das Gewürzkrämer-Kleeblatt*]. *Der Sammler*, 1 March 1845 (no. 34): 134-35.

Schindler, F[ranz] V. 1845. [Review of *Das Gewürzkrämer-Kleeblatt*]. *Oesterreichisches Morgenblatt*, 1 March 1845 (no. 26): 102-3.

Herlosssohn, K[arl]; H[ermann] Marggraff, *et al.*, eds. 1846. "Nestroy." *Allgemeines Theater-Lexikon oder Encyklopädie alles Wissenswerthen für Bühnenkünstler, Dilettanten und Theaterfreunde*. New edition. 7 vols. Altenburg, Leipzig: Expedition des Theater-Lexikons. 1839-46. 5: 352-53 (signed "E. St.").

Adami, H[einrich]. 1846. [Review of *Der Unbedeutende*]. *Theaterzeitung*, 5 May 1846 (no. 107): 426.

Hamerling, Robert [1846]. [Diary entry, 18 June 1846]. Reprinted in Hüttner 1982: 55-56.

Arnold, K. 1847a. "Ueber den Verfall der Volkstheater." *Oesterreichische Blätter für Literatur und Kunst, Geografie, Geschichte, Statistik und Naturkunde*. 30 March 1847 (no. 76): 301-2.

Breier, Eduard. 1847. "Das Lokalstück, Nestroy und sein 'Schützling'." *Wiener Zeitschrift für Kunst, Literatur, Theater und Mode*, 10 April 1847 (no. 72): 286-87; 12 April 1847 (no. 73): 290-91.

Adami, H[einrich]. 1847. "Nestroys neue Posse: 'Der Schützling'." *Allgemeine Theaterzeitung*, 12 April 1847 (no. 87): 346.

Norbert, E. 1847. [Review of *Der Schützling*]. *Die Gegenwart*, 12 April 1847 (no. 83): 386-87.

Raudnitz, L. 1847. "Die neue Richtung der Nestroyschen Muse und sein 'Schützling'." *Allgemeine Theaterzeitung*, 13 April 1847 (no. 88): 350.

Schindler, F[ranz] V. 1847. [Review of *Der Schützling*]. *Oesterreichisches Morgenblatt*, 14 April 1847 (no. 45): 178-79.

Arnold, C. 1847b. "Wiener dramaturgische Berichte." *Oesterreichische Blätter für Literatur und Kunst, Geografie, Geschichte, Statistik und Naturkunde*, 17 April 1847 (no. 92): 365-66.

Saphir, M. G. 1847a. "Des Wiener Volksstücks Glück und Ende." *Der Humorist*, 12-13 May 1847 (no. 113-14): 449-51; 15 May 1847 (no. 116): 461-62; 17 May 1847 (no. 117): 465-68.

Gutt, Bernhard. 1847a. [Review of *Der Schützling*]. *Bohemia*, 20 May (no. 80) and 21 May (no. 81).

Gutt, Bernhard. 1847b. [Review of Nestroy's fourth appearance in *Der Schützling* in Prague]. *Bohemia*, 27 May 1847 (no. 84).

Hebbel, Friedrich. 1847. Diary, 28-29 June 1847. Reprinted in Hebbel, *Sämtliche Werke*, ed. by Richard Maria Werner. 24 vols. Berlin: B. Behr. 1901-7. Part 2, 3: 246-51.

W. 1847. "Der Zerrissene, von J. Nestroy." *Didaskalia. Blätter für Geist, Gemüth und Publizität* (Frankfurt a.M.), 11 September 1847 (no. 251).

Saphir, M.G. 1847b. "Der Rezensent in dem Gasluster des neuen Carl-Theaters." *Der Humorist*, 15 December 1847 (no. 299): 1193-95; 16 December 1847 (no. 300): 1197-99.

März. 1848. [Review of *Die Freiheit in Krähwinkel*]. *Der Humorist*, 3 July 1848 (no. 158): 655. (Reprinted in *Johann Nestroys gesammelte Briefe (1831-1862). Nestroy und seine Bühne im Jahre 1848*, ed. Fritz Brukner. Vienna: Wallishausser. 1938. 112-13.)

Anon. 1848. *Nestroy und die Freiheit in Krähwinkel*. Vienna: J. N. Friedrich. (Reprinted in *Johann Nestroys gesammelte Briefe (1831-1862). Nestroy und seine Bühne im Jahre 1848*, ed. Fritz Brukner. Vienna: Wallishausser. 1938. 113-16.)

Hebbel, Friedrich. 1848. "Belagerung von Wien." *Allgemeine Zeitung* (Stuttgart and Augsburg), 22 October 1848 (no. 296). Reprinted in Hebbel, *Sämtliche Werke*, ed. by Richard Maria Werner. 24 vols. Berlin: B. Behr. 1901-7. Part 1, 10: 131-35.

Hebbel, Friedrich. 1849. "Das 'Versprechen hinter'm Heerd' im Burgtheater." *Die Presse*, 12 January 1849 (no. 10). Reprinted in Hebbel, *Sämtliche Werke*, ed. by Richard Maria Werner. 24 vols. Berlin: B. Behr. 1901-7. Part 1, 11: 260-65.

X. Rdl. 1852. [Review of *Kampl*]. *Wiener allgemeine Zeitung* [= *Theaterzeitung*], 31 March 1852 (no. 75): 303. (Reprinted *HKA: Stücke 31*: 185-87.)

Bauernfeld, Eduard von. 1853. "Die Wiener Volksbühne," 2. *Österreichische Blätter für Literatur und Kunst. Beilage zur Wiener Zeitung*, 25 April 1853: 99-101.

Kaiser, Friedrich. 1854. *Theater-Director Carl. Sein Leben und Wirken — in München und Wien, mit einer entwickelten Schilderung seines Charakters und seiner Stellung zur Volksbühne*. Vienna: Sallmayer.

Silberstein, August. 1861. "Nestroy." *Oesterreichische Zeitung*, 21 February 1861 (no. 46): [1].

Vischer, Friedrich Theodor. [1861]. "Eine Reise." Reprinted in Friedrich Theodor Vischer, *Kritische Gänge*. 2nd revised edition, ed. Robert Vischer. 2 vols. Leipzig: Verlag der Weißen Bücher. 1914. 1: 309-450.

Hebbel, Friedrich. 1862a. Wiener Briefe, [9]. *Illustrirte Zeitung* (Leipzig), 15 February 1862 (no. 972). Reprinted in Hebbel, *Sämtliche Werke*, ed. by Richard Maria Werner. 24 vols. Berlin: B. Behr. 1901-7. Part 1, 10: 272-78.

Anon. 1862. "From our own Correspondent" [dated: Vienna, June 6]. *The Times* (London), 10 June 1862: 12.

Kuh, Emil. 1862. "Aristophanes-Nestroy" (signed "Em.K."). *Die Presse*, 15 June 1862 (no. 163): 1-3.

Hebbel, Friedrich. 1862b. Wiener Briefe, [13]. *Illustrirte Zeitung* (Leipzig), 11 October 1862 (no. 1006). Reprinted in Hebbel, *Sämtliche Werke*, ed. by Richard Maria Werner. 24 vols. Berlin: B. Behr. 1901-7. Part 1, 10: 292-301.

Wurzbach, Constant von. 1869. *Biographisches Lexikon des Kaiserthums Oesterreich*. 60 vols. Vienna: L. C. Zamarski [Vol 1]; Verlag der typographisch-literarisch-artistischen Anstalt [vols 2-5]; Verlag der k.k. Hof- und Staatsdruckerei [vols 6-61]. 1856-91. 20: 204-25: "Nestroy, Johann."

Kaiser, Friedrich. 1870. *Unter fünfzehn Theater-Direktoren. Bunte Bilder* aus der Wiener Bühnenwelt. Vienna: Waldheim.

Holtei, Karl von. 1872. "[Raimund und Nestroy]." In Holtei, *Simmelsammelsurium aus Briefen, gedruckten Büchern, aus dem Leben und aus ihm selbst*. 2 vols. Breslau: Trewendt. 1: 286-96. Reprinted in Karl von Holtei, *Ausgewählte Werke*, ed. Jürgen Hein and Henk J. Koning. Vol. 1: *Gedichte, Lieder, Stücke, Schriften zu Literatur und Theater*. Würzburg: Bergstadtverlag Wilhelm Gottlieb Korn. 1992: 397-404.

Reschauer, Heinrich. 1872. Heinrich Reschauer and Moritz Smets, *Das Jahr 1848. Geschichte der Wiener Revolution*. 2 vols. Vienna: Waldheim. Volume 1.

Bauernfeld, Eduard von. 1873. "Aus Alt- und Neu-Wien." In Bauernfeld, *Gesammelte Schriften*. 12 vols. Vienna: Braumüller. 1871-73. Volume 12.

Wagner, Richard. 1873. Censuren, 5: "Aufklärungen über das Judenthum in der Musik" (Letter to Frau Marie Muchanoff, 1869). In Richard Wagner, *Gesammelte Schriften und Dichtungen*. 10 vols. Leipzig: Fritzsch. 1871-83. 8: 299-323.

Laube, Heinrich. [1875-80]. *Erinnerungen 1810-1840*. Reprinted in Laube, *Gesammelte Werke*, ed. Heinrich Hubert Houben. 50 vols. Leipzig: Hesse. 1908-9. 40: 1-424.

Speidel, Ludwig. 1881. "Johann Nestroy" (signed "L.Sp."). *Neue Freie Presse*, 16 January 1881 (no. 5885): 1-2. Reprinted in Speidel, *Persönlichkeiten*. Biographisch-literarische Essays. (Speidel, *Schriften*, 1). Berlin: Meyer & Jessen. 1910. 128-35.

Schlögl, Friedrich. [1883]. *Vom Wiener Volkstheater. Erinnerungen und Aufzeichnungen*. Vienna, Teschen: Prochaska. 144-53: "Johann Nestroy."

Werner, R. M. 1886. Article "Nestroy" in *Allgemeine deutsche Biographie*, 56 vols, Leipzig: Duncker und Humblot. 1875-1912. 23: 447-55.

Speidel, Ludwig. 1888. "Theater." In *Wien 1848-1888. Denkschrift zum 2. December 1888*. 2 vols. Vienna: Konegen. 2: 343-408.

Necker, Moritz. 1891. *Johann Nestroy. Eine biographisch-kritische Skizze. Johann Nestroy's Gesammelte Werke*, ed. Vincenz Chiavacci and Ludwig Ganghofer. 12 vols. Stuttgart: Bonz 1890-91 (*CG*). 12: 93-218.

Bahr, Hermann. 1899. *Wiener Theater (1892-1898)*. Berlin: S. Fischer.

Sittenberger, Hans. 1901. "Johann Nestroy." *Jahrbuch der Grillparzer-Gesellschaft* 11: 125-64.

Hock, Stefan. 1905. "Von Raimund bis Anzengruber. Eine literarhistorische Skizze." *Jahrbuch der Grillparzer-Gesellschaft* 15: 31-60.

Leixner, Otto von. 1906. *Geschichte der Deutschen Literatur*. 7th edition. Leipzig: Spamer.

Zeidler, Jakob. 1907. "Die Grundlagen von Johann Nestroys literarischer Eigenart und Weltanschauung." *Die Kultur* 8, no. 4: 433-48.

Kraus, Karl. 1908. "Der Fürstentag." *Die Fackel* 254-255: 1-4.

Rosner, Leopold. 1910. *Schatten aus dem alten Wien. Erinnerungen*, ed. Karl Rosner. Berlin: Meyer & Jessen. 161-74: "Johann Nestroy."

Kosch, Wilhelm. 1912. "Das Volksstück von Raimund bis Anzengruber." *Zeitschrift für den deutschen Unterricht*. 26: 16-28.

Berger, Alfred von. 1912. "Johann Nestroy. (Zu Nestroys fünfzigstem Geburtstag)." *Neue Freie Presse*, 26 May 1912 (no. 17154). Pfingstbeilage: 31-32.

Blasel, Karl. 1912. "Johann Nepomuk Nestroy." *Neue Freie Presse*, 28 May 1912, Nachmittagsblatt (no. 17155): 1-2.

Kraus, Karl. 1912a. "Nestroy und die Nachwelt. Zum 50. Todestage." *Die Fackel* 349-350: 1-23.

Kraus, Karl. 1912b. "Nestroy-Feier." *Die Fackel* 351-353: 28-47.

Kraus, Karl. 1917. "Die Literaturlüge auf dem Theater." *Die Fackel* 457-461: 53-57.

Enzinger, Moriz. 1918-19. *Die Entwicklung des Wiener Theaters vom 16. zum 19. Jahrhundert (Stoffe und Motive)*. Schriften der Gesellschaft für Theatergeschichte, 28-29. Berlin: Gesellschaft für Theatergeschichte.

Kraus, Karl. 1921. "Die Wortgestalt." *Die Fackel* 572-576: 69-74.

Meyer, Richard M. 1921. *Geschichte der deutschen Literatur*, 2. Bd.: *Die deutsche Literatur des 19. und 20. Jahrhunderts*. 6th edition, ed. and continued by Hugo Bieber. Berlin: Bondi.

Kraus, Karl. 1922a. "Grillparzer-Feier." *Die Fackel* 588-594: 12-21.

Kraus, Karl. 1922b. "Nestroy und die Literaten." *Die Fackel* 595-600: 53-55.

Kraus, Karl. 1922c. "Vorlesungen." *Die Fackel*. 595-600: 64-82.

Arnold, Robert F. 1923. "Eine Nestroy-Quelle." *Das   Literarische Echo 25: 1148.*

Holl, Karl. 1923. *Geschichte des deutschen Lustspiels.* Leipzig: Weber.

Kraus, Karl. 1923. "Nestroy-Zyklus." *Die Fackel* 613-621: 42-58.

Kraus, Karl. 1924. "Ein zeitgenössischer Kritiker Nestroys." *Die Fackel* 657-667: 100-20.

Kraus, Karl. 1925. "Nestroy und das Burgtheater." *Die Fackel* 676-678: 1-40.

Liegler, Leopold, ed. 1925a. *Eine Wohnung ist zu vermieten.* Johannn Nestroy, *Ausgewählte Werke,* 3. Vienna: Lányi.

Liegler, Leopold. 1925b. "Johann Nestroy. Ein charakterologischer Versuch." *Die Wage* (New Series) 6, no. 1 (7 March 1925): 18-26.

Hadamowsky, Franz. 1926. "Das Carltheater unter der Direktion Johann Nestroys." *Jahrbuch der österreichischen Leo-Gesellschaft:* 196-241.

Rommel, Otto. 1926. "Nestroys Volksstücke. (Begründung der Auswahl)." Nestroy, *Sämtliche Werke,* ed. Fritz Brukner and Otto Rommel. 15 vols. Vienna: Schroll. 1924-30 (*SW*). 8: 556-65.

Liegler, Leopold. 1930. "Johann Nestroy. Ein Bild der Zeit und der Persönlichkeit." *Die Freyung,* no. 1 (March 1930): 3-20.

Rommel, Otto. 1930. *Johann Nestroy. Ein Beitrag zur Geschichte der Wiener Volkskomik.* Nestroy, *Sämtliche Werke,* ed. Fritz Brukner and Otto Rommel. 15 vols. Vienna: Schroll. 1924-30 (*SW*). Volume 15.

Bietak, Wilhelm. 1931. *Das Lebensgefühl des "Biedermeier" in der österreichischen Dichtung.* Vienna, Leipzig: Braumüller. 129-44.

Friedell, Egon. 1931. *Kulturgeschichte der Neuzeit. Die Krisis der europäischen Seele von der schwarzen Pest bis zum Weltkrieg.* 3 vols. Munich: C. H. Beck. 1927-31. 3: *Romantik und Liberalismus / Imperialismus und Impressionismus.*

Mautner, Franz Heinrich. 1931. "Das Wortspiel und seine Bedeutung. Grundzüge der geistesgeschichtlichen Darstellung eines Sprachelementes." *Deutsche Vierteljahrsschrift für Literaturwissenschaft und Geistesgeschichte* 9: 679-710.

Forst de Battaglia, Otto. 1932. *Johann Nestroy. Abschätzer der Menschen, Magier des Wortes.* Leipzig: Staackmann.

Katann, Otto. 1932. *Gesetz im Wandel. Neue literarische Studien.* Innsbruck, Vienna, Munich: Tyrolia. 92-100: "Nestroys Posse *Der Zerrissene.*"

Bührmann, Max. 1933. "Johann Nepomuk Nestroys Parodien." Diss. Kiel. Kiel: Buchdruckerei Schmidt & Klaunig.

Körner, Josef. 1933. [Review of Forst de Battaglia 1932]. *Deutsche Literaturzeitung,* no. 32: cols 1510-13.

Hadamowsky, Franz. 1934. *Das Theater in der Wiener Leopoldstadt 1781-1860* (Kataloge der Theatersammlung der Nationalbibliothek in Wien, 3). Vienna: Höfels.

Stoessl, Otto. 1935. *Geist und Gehalt*. Vienna: Saturn-Verlag. 218-40: "Nestroy."

Feder, Fritz [= Jura Soyfer]. 1937. "Vom lebendigen Nestroy. Zum 75. Todestag." *Der Wiener Tag*, 20 May 1937 (no. 167). Reprinted in Jura Soyfer, *Das Gesamtwerk*, ed. Horst Jarka. Vienna, Munich, Zürich: Europaverlag. 1980: 469-73.

Fontana, Oskar Maurus. 1937.[Review of production of *Der Talisman*]. *Der Wiener Tag*. 26 September 1937 (no. 5132): 8-9. Reprinted *HKA: Stücke* 17/i: 182-83.

Mautner, Franz H. [1937]. *Johann Nestroy und seine Kunst*. Vienna: Otto Lorenz.

Friess, H. 1940-41. "Nestroys schauspielerische Tätigkeit in Graz im Spiegel der zeitgenössischen Kritik." *Die Städtischen Bühnen Graz*, Programmheft 7: 73-77.

Wallner, Anton. 1941. "Die Quellen zweier Komödien Nestroy's." *Dichtung und Volkstum* [= *Euphorion*] 41: 496-500.

Gregor, Joseph. 1943. *Das Theater des Volkes in der Ostmark*. Vienna: Jugend und Volk.

Liebl, Zeno von. 1943. [Review of première of *"Nur keck!"*]. *Neues Wiener Tagblatt*, 4 July 1943 (no. 182): 3. (Reprinted *HKA: Stücke 34*, 132-33.)

Bauer, Anton. 1944. "Die Musik in den Theaterstücken Johann Nestroys. Ein Beitrag zur volkstümlichen Theatermusik Wiens." *Jahrbuch der Gesellschaft für Wiener Theaterforschung 1944*: 132-48.

Bujak, Liselotte. 1948. "Nestroys Beziehungen zum Biedermeier." Diss. Vienna.

Rommel, Otto. 1948. "Johann Nestroy. Der Satiriker auf der Altwiener Komödienbühne." In Nestroy, *Gesammelte Werke*, ed. Otto Rommel. 6 vols. Vienna: Schroll (*GW*). 1: 5-193.

Rommel, Otto. 1949. "Die Theaterlyrik Nestroys und ihre künstlerische Entwicklung." In Nestroy, *Gesammelte Werke*, ed. Otto Rommel. 6 vols. Vienna: Schroll (*GW*). 6: 586-605.

Nadler, Josef. 1951. *Literaturgeschichte Österreichs*. 2nd edition. Salzburg: Otto Müller. 310-12.

Weigel, Hans. 1951. "Johann Nestroy oder: Die Kunst und ihr Gegenstand." *Der Monat* 4: 303-13.

Rommel, Otto. 1952. *Die Alt-Wiener Volkskomödie. Ihre Geschichte vom barocken Welt-Theater bis zum Tode Nestroys*. Vienna: Schroll. 927-75: "Johann Nestroy: Das Alt-Wiener Lokalstück wird große Satire."

Haas, Willy. 1952. "Blick auf Nestroy." *Merkur* 6, no. 11 (November): 1084-89.

Greiner, Martin. 1954. *Zwischen Biedermeier und Bourgeoisie. Ein Kapitel deutscher Literaturgeschichte im Zeichen Heinrich Heines.* Leipzig: Koehler & Amelang. 30-50.

Schick, Paul. 1956. "Der Satiriker und der Tod. Versuch einer typologischen Deutung." In *Festschrift zum hundertjährigen Bestehen der Wiener Stadtbibliothek 1856-1956.* Wiener Schriften, 4. Vienna: Jugend und Volk. 200-31.

Reichert, Herbert W. 1957. "Some Causes of the Nestroy Renaissance in Vienna." *Monatshefte* 47: 221-30.

Mautner, Franz H. 1958. "Nestroy, *Der Talisman.*" In *Das deutsche Drama vom Barock bis zur Gegenwart. Interpretationen,* ed. Benno von Wiese. 2 vols. Düsseldorf: Bagel. 2: 23-42. Reprinted: Mautner 1974a: 66-91. (Notes 349-50.)

Barraclough, Clifford A. 1960. "Nestroy, the Political Satirist." *Monatshefte für deutschen Unterricht, deutsche Sprache und Literatur* 52: 253-57.

Weigel, Hans. 1960. *Flucht vor der Größe. Beiträge zur Erkenntnis und Selbsterkenntnis Österreichs.* Vienna: Wollzeilen Verlag. 73-100: "Johann Nestroy oder Die Flucht in die Vorstadt."

Weigel, Hans. 1961. *Tausendundeine Premiere. Wiener Theater 1946-1961.* Vienna: Wollzeilen Verlag.

Esslin, Martin. 1962. *The Theatre of the Absurd.* London: Eyre and Spottiswoode.

Fischer, Ernst. 1962. "Johann Nestroy. Zu seinem hundertsten Todestag." *Sinn und Form* 14 (1962): 430-481. Reprinted in Ernst Fischer, *Von Grillparzer zu Kafka. Sechs Essays.* suhrkamp taschenbuch, 284. Stuttgart: Suhrkamp 1975. 145-242: "Johann Nestroy."

Fontana, Oskar Maurus. 1962. "Die Wiener Grillparzer-, Raimund- und Nestroy-Neuaufführungen seit 1945." *Maske und Kothurn* 8: 132-41.

Forst de Battaglia, Otto. 1962. *Johann Nestroy.* Munich: Langen-Müller.

Gengnagel, Dagmar. 1962. "Zur sprachlichen Gestaltung der Possen Johann Nestroys." *Wissenschaftliche Zeitschrift der Friedrich–Schiller–Universität Jena* 11. Gesellschafts- und Sprachwissenschaftliche Reihe, no. 1: 119-30.

Mautner, Franz H. 1963. "Nestroys Kunst und unsere Zeit." *Jahrbuch der deutschen Schillergesellschaft* 7: 383-415.

Plard, Henri. 1963. "Du sublime au ridicule: Hebbel et Nestroy." *Études Germaniques* 18: 397-418.

Eisenreich, Herbert. 1964. *Reaktionen. Essays zur Literatur.* Gütersloh: S. Mohn: 227-45: "Nestroy oder 'Ich hätt' sollen g'scheiter sein'."

Hüttner, Johann. 1964. "Wiener Nestroyaufführungen vom Tode des Autors bis zum Ende des zweiten Weltkrieges." 2 vols. Diss. Vienna.

Bauer, Roger. 1965. *La Réalité, royaume de Dieu. Études sur l'originalité du théâtre viennois dans la première moitié du XIXe siècle*. Munich: Hueber. 175-256.

Kuhn, Christoph. [1966]. *Witz und Weltanschauung in Nestroys Auftrittsmonologen*. Zürich: Juris-Verlag.

Reimann, Paul. 1966. "Einleitung." In Johann Nestroy, *Werke in zwei Bänden*. 2 vols. 2nd edition. Berlin and Weimar: Aufbau. 1: v-xxxiv.

Torberg, Friedrich. 1966. *Das fünfte Rad am Thespiskarren. Theaterkritiken*. Munich and Vienna: Langen-Müller.

Basil, Otto. 1967. *Johann Nestroy in Selbstzeugnissen und Bilddokumenten*. rororo bildmonographien, 132. Reinbek bei Hamburg: Rowohlt.

Brill, Siegfried. 1967. *Die Komödie der Sprache. Untersuchungen zum Werke Johann Nestroys*. Erlanger Beiträge zur Sprach- und Kunstwissenschaft, 28. Nürnberg: Hans Carl.

Hillach, Ansgar. 1967. *Die Dramatisierung des komischen Dialogs. Figur und Rolle bei Nestroy*. Munich: Fink.

Gladt, Karl. 1967. *Die Handschriften Johann Nestroys*. Graz, Vienna, Cologne: Böhlau.

Bauer, Roger. 1968. "J. N. Nestroy: *Einen Jux will er sich machen*." *Études Germaniques* 23: 367-80.

Boege, Günther. 1968. "Nestroy als Bearbeiter. Studien zu *Die verhängnisvolle Faschingsnacht*, *Der Unbedeutende* und *Judith und Holofernes*." Diss. Frankfurt a.M.

Hein, Jürgen. 1968. "Nestroyforschung (1901-1966)." *Wirkendes Wort* 18: 232-45.

Preisner, Rio. 1968. *Johann Nepomuk Nestroy. Der Schöpfer der tragischen Posse*. Munich: Hanser.

Yates, W. E. 1968. "Nestroysche Stilelemente bei Anzengruber. Ein Beitrag zur Wirkungsgeschichte der Possen Nestroys." *Maske und Kothurn* 14: 287-96.

Diehl, Siegfried. 1969. *Zauberei und Satire im Frühwerk Nestroys. Mit neuen Handschriften zum "Konfusen Zauberer" und zum "Zauberer Sulphur."* Frankfurter Beiträge zur Germanistik, 9. Bad Homburg v.d.H.: Gehlen.

Herles, Helmut. 1969. "Das Theaterereignis der Saison. Nestroy und sein Frankfurter Gastspiel im Jahre 1847 / Seine Stücke waren schon bekannt." *Frankfurter Allgemeine Zeitung*, 21 June 1969 (no. 140): 27.

Preisendanz, Wolfgang. 1969. "Nestroys komisches Theater." In *Das deutsche Lustspiel*, ed. Hans Steffen. 2 vols. Göttingen: Vandenhoeck & Ruprecht. 1968-69. 2: 7-24.

Tönz, Leo. 1969. *Die künstlerische Eigenständigkeit und Eigenart Nestroys*. Dissertationen der Universität Wien, 31. Vienna: Notring.

Haeberle, Erwin J. 1970. "Nestroy oder Der gerade Umweg der Satire." *Neue Rundschau* 81: 302-14.

Hein, Jürgen. 1970. *Spiel und Satire in der Komödie Johann Nestroys*. Bad Homburg v.d.H.: Gehlen.

Kahl, Kurt. 1970. *Johann Nestroy oder Der wienerische Shakespeare*. Vienna: Molden.

Barlow, John D. 1971. [Review of Diehl 1969 and Tönz 1969]. *Monatshefte* 63: 88-90.

Branscombe, Peter. 1971-72. "Music in the Viennese Popular Theatre of the Eighteenth and Nineteenth Centuries." *Proceedings of the Royal Musical Association* 98: 101-12.

Arntzen, Helmut. 1972. "Dementi einer Tragödie. Zu Hebbels und Nestroys *Judith*." *Studi Germanici* 10: 405-23.

Destro, Alberto. 1972. *L'Intelligenza come struttura drammatica. Saggio su Johann Nestroy*. Naples: Istituto Universitario Orientale.

Hilmar, Ernst. 1972. "Die Nestroy-Vertonungen in den Wiener Sammlungen." *Maske und Kothurn* 18: 38-98.

Preisner, Rio. 1972. "Der konservative Nestroy. Aspekte der zukünftigen Forschung." *Maske und Kothurn* 18: 23-37.

Walla, Friedrich. 1972 [submitted 1969]. "Untersuchungen zur dramatischen Technik Johann Nestroys." Diss. Vienna.

Weigel, Hans. 1972. *Johann Nestroy*. Friedrichs Dramatiker des Welttheaters, 27. 2nd edition. Velber bei Hannover: Friedrich.

Yates, W. E. 1972. *Nestroy: Satire and Parody in Viennese Popular Comedy*. Cambridge: Cambridge University Press.

Denkler, Horst. 1973. *Restauration und Revolution. Politische Tendenzen im deutschen Drama zwischen Wiener Kongreß und Märzrevolution*. Munich: Fink.

Eder, Alois. 1973a. "Literarische Sozialkritik im Vormärz. Nestroys Werk als Quelle der Sozialgeschichte." *Beiträge zur historischen Sozialkunde* 3, no. 3: 48-53.

Hein, Jürgen, ed. 1973. *Theater und Gesellschaft. Das Volksstück im 19. und 20. Jahrhundert*. Literatur in der Gesellschaft, 12. Düsseldorf: Bertelsmann Universitätsverlag.

Includes:

Eder, Alois. 1973b. "'Die geistige Kraft der Gemeinheit.' Zur Sozialgeschichte der Rezeption Nestroys." 133-53.

Herles, Helmut. 1973a. "Nestroy und die Zensur." 121-32.

Herles, Helmut. 1973b. "Nestroy im Norden. Anmerkungen zur Wirkungsgeschichte." 155-59.

Mautner, Franz H. 1973. "Geld, Nestroy und Nestroy-Interpretation." 113-19.

McKenzie, John R. P. 1973. "The Technique of *Verwienerung* in Nestroy's *Judith und Holofernes*." *New German Studies* 1: 119-32.

Urbach, Reinhard. 1973. *Die Wiener Volkskomödie und ihr Publikum. Stranitzky und die Folgen*. Vienna, Munich: Jugend und Volk. 117-25.

Bruckner, John Peroutka. 1973. "An Annotated Nestroy Bibliography." Diss. University of Virginia.

Harding, Laurence V. 1974. *The Dramatic Art of Ferdinand Raimund and Johann Nestroy*. The Hague: Mouton.

Helmensdorfer, Urs. 1974. "Nestroys politisches Testament. *Der alte Mann mit der jungen Frau*." *Neue Zürcher Zeitung*, 23-24 November 1974 (no. 499): 67-68.

Herles, Helmut. 1974. *Nestroys Komödie: "Der Talisman": Von der ersten Notiz zum vollendeten Werk. Mit bisher unveröffentlichten Handschriften*. Munich: Fink.

Mautner, Franz H. 1974a. *Wort und Wesen. Kleine Schriften zur Literatur und Sprache*. Frankfurt a.M.: Insel. 92-97: "Über Nestroys *Der Färber und sein Zwillingsbruder*." (Notes 350.)

Mautner, Franz H. 1974b. *Nestroy*. Heidelberg: Stiehm.

Hein, Jürgen. 1975. "Neuere Nestroyforschung (1967-1973)." *Wirkendes Wort* 25: 140-51.

Hüttner, Johann. 1975. "Nestroy ohne Nestroy auf dem Theater." *Neue Zürcher Zeitung*, 1-2 November 1975 (no. 254): 51.

Kudzus, Winfried, and Hinrich C. Seeba, eds. 1975. *Austriaca. Beiträge zur österreichischen Literatur. Festschrift für Heinz Politzer zum 65. Geburtstag*. Tübingen: Niemeyer.

Includes:

Jens, Walter. 1975. "Johann Nestroy." 148-50.

Seeba, Hinrich C. 1975. "Die Sprache der Freiheit in Krähwinkel." 127-47.

May, Erich Joachim. 1975. *Wiener Volkskomödie und Vormärz*. Berlin: Henschelverlag.

Branscombe, Peter. 1976. "The Connexions between Drama and Music in the Viennese Popular Theatre from the Opening of the Leopoldstädter Theater (1781) to Nestroy's Opera Parodies (ca. 1855), with Special Reference to the Forms of Parody." Diss. University of London.

Rogers, Michael Anthony. 1976. "Elements of Convention and Theatricality in the Works of Johann Nestroy." Diss. University of Cambridge.

Stierle, Karlheinz. 1976. "Komik der Handlung, Komik der Sprachhandlung, Komik der Komödie." In *Das Komische*, ed. Wolfgang Preisendanz and Rainer Warning. Munich: Fink. 237-68.

Matt, Peter von. 1976. "Nestroys Panik." *Tagesanzeiger* (Zürich), Magazin 48 (27 November 1976): 7-17.

Bauer, Roger. 1976. "Nestroy und Frankreich." *Neue Zürcher Zeitung*, 4-5 December 1976 (no. 285): 67.

Bauer, Roger. 1977. *Laßt sie koaxen, Die kritischen Frösch' in Preußen und Sachsen! Zwei Jahrhunderte Literatur in Österreich*. Vienna: Europaverlag. 136-49: "Nestroys 'Jux' oder die Wandlung einer englischen Komödie zum Wiener Volksstück." (Notes 248-89.)

Berghaus, Günter. 1977. "J. N. Nestroys Revolutionspossen im Rahmen des Gesamtwerks. Ein Beitrag zur Bestimmung von Nestroys Weltanschauung auf dem Hintergrund der österreichischen Sozialgeschichte des Vormärz." Diss. Freie Universität Berlin.

Hannemann, Bruno. 1977. *Johann Nestroy. Nihilistisches Welttheater und verflixter Kerl. Zum Ende der Wiener Komödie*. Abhandlungen zur Kunst-, Musik- und Literaturwissenschaft, 215. Bonn: Bouvier.

Hüttner, Johann. 1977. "Johann Nestroy im Theaterbetrieb seiner Zeit." *Maske und Kothurn* 23: 233-43.

Pütz, Peter. 1977. "Zwei Krähwinkeliaden 1802/1848. Kotzebue: *Die deutschen Kleinstädter*, Nestroy: *Freiheit in Krähwinkel*." In *Die deutsche Komödie. Vom Mittelalter bis zur Gegenwart*, ed. Walter Hinck. Düsseldorf: Bagel. 175-94. (Notes 385-86.)

Yates, W. E. 1977. "Playing to the Gallery." *The Times Literary Supplement*, 3 June 1977 (no. 3925): 687.

Hein, Jürgen. 1978. *Das Wiener Volkstheater. Raimund und Nestroy*. Erträge der Forschung, 100. Darmstadt: Wissenschaftliche Buchgesellschaft.

Rogers, M. A. 1978. "'Dies Österreich ist eine kleine Welt'." In *Austrian Life and Literature 1780-1938. Eight Essays*, ed. Peter Branscombe. Edinburgh: Scottish Academic Press. 72-79.

Slobodkin, G. S. 1978. "Nestroy und die Tradition des Volkstheaters im Schaffen Brechts." Translated by Manfred Abendroth. *Weimarer Beiträge* 24, no. 9: 99-117.

Yates, W. E. 1978. "An Object of Nestroy's Satire. Friedrich Kaiser and the *Lebensbild*." *Renaissance and Modern Studies* 22: 45-62.

Apel, Friedmar. 1979. "Komische Melancholie, lustige Entfremdung. Zur Struktur der Komik im neueren Lustspiel." *Sprache im technischen Zeitalter* 70: 145-70.

Corriher, Kurt. 1979. "Nestroy and Individual Identity." *Germanic Review* 54: 160-64.

Hüttner, Johann. 1979. "Machte sich Nestroy bezahlt?" *Nestroyana* 1: 3-15.

Müller, Gerd. 1979. *Das Volksstück von Raimund bis Kroetz. Die Gattung in Einzelanalysen.* Munich: Oldenbourg. 26-41.

Müller-Dietz, Heinz. 1979. "Alltagsmoral und Alltagskriminalität. Zur skeptischen Weltsicht Johann Nestroys." In *Festschrift für Paul Bockelmann zum 70. Geburtstag am 7. Dezember 1978*, ed. Arthur Kaufmann, Günter Bemmann, Detlev Krauss, and Klaus Volk. Munich: C. H. Beck 1979: 21-43. Reprinted in Müller-Dietz, Heinz: *Grenzüberschreitungen. Beiträge zur Beziehung zwischen Literatur und Recht.* Baden-Baden: Nomos 1990. 281-302.

Neuber, Wolfgang. 1979. "Ein Fund unbekannter Nestroy-Handschriften." *Jahrbuch des Wiener Goethe-Vereins* 81-83 [1977-79]: 315-20.

Walla, Friedrich. 1979a. "Johann Nestroys Spiel mit der Biographie: *Der Tod am Hochzeitstage oder Mann, Frau, Kind*." *Seminar* 15: 97-113.

Walla, Friedrich. 1979b. "Die menschliche Tragödie: Johann Nestroys *Der Tod am Hochzeitstage oder Mann, Frau, Kind*." *Nestroyana* 1: 41-61.

Yates, W. Edgar. 1979. "Nestroys Komödie der Freundschaft: *Der Zerrissene*." *Österreich in Geschichte und Literatur* 23: 43-48.

Draudt, Manfred. 1980. "'Der unzusammenhängende Zusammenhang': Johann Nestroy und William Shakespeare. Dramatische Konventionen im Wiener Volkstheater und im elisabethanischen Public Theatre." *Maske und Kothurn* 26: 16-58.

Hein, Jürgen. 1980. "Nestroys Possen im Rahmen der Vormärz-Dramaturgie." *Nestroyana* 2: 38-49.

Hüttner, Johann. 1980a. "Theatre Censorship in Metternich's Vienna." *Theatre Quarterly* 10, no. 37: 61-69.

Hüttner, Johann. 1980b. "*Der Treulose* — ein Fall für die Nestroyforschung." *Nestroyana* 2: 61-71.

Hüttner, Johann. 1980c. "Selbstzensur bei Johann Nestroy." *Die Presse* (Vienna), 13-14 September 1980, Literaricum: 4-5.

Hüttner, Johann. 1980d. "Vor- und Selbstzensur bei Johann Nestroy." *Maske und Kothurn* 26: 234-48.

Jansen, Peter K. 1980. "Johann Nepomuk Nestroys skeptische Utopie. Märchen und Wirklichkeit in *Der Talisman*." *Jahrbuch der deutschen Schillergesellschaft* 24: 247-82.

Klotz, Volker. 1980. *Bürgerliches Lachtheater. Komödie, Posse, Schwank, Operette.* Munich: Deutscher Taschenbuch Verlag. 45-63.

McKenzie, John R. P. 1980. "Political Satire in Nestroy's *Freiheit in Krähwinkel*." *Modern Language Review* 75: 322-32.

Sengle, Friedrich. 1980. *Biedermeierzeit. Deutsche Literatur im Spannungsfeld zwischen Restauration und Revolution 1815-1848.* 3 vols. Stuttgart. Metzler 1971-80. 3: 191-264: "Johann Nestroy (1801-1862)." (Notes 1090-93.)

Baur, Uwe. 1981. "Nestroy und die oppositionelle Literatur seiner Zeit. Zum Verhältnis von 'Volk' und Literatur in der Restaurationsepoche." *Studien zur Literatur des 19. und 20. Jahrhunderts in Österreich. Festschrift für Alfred Doppler zum 60. Geburtstag*, ed. Johann Holzner *et al.* Innsbrucker Beiträge zur Kulturwissenschaft, Germanistische Reihe, 12. Innsbruck: Institut für Germanistik an der Universität Innsbruck. 25-34.

Corriher, Kurt. 1981. "The Conflict between Dignity and Hope in the Works of Johann Nestroy." *South Atlantic Review* 46, no. 2: 27-42.

Hüttner, Johann. 1981. "Das theatrale Umfeld Nestroys." *Nestroyana* 3: 140-55.

Rössler, Helmut. 1981. *Karl Kraus und Nestroy. Kritik und Verarbeitung.* Stuttgarter Arbeiten zur Germanistik, 90. Stuttgart: Heinz.

Scheck, Ulrich. 1981. *Parodie und Eigenständigkeit in Nestroys 'Judith* und *Holofernes.' Ein Vergleich mit Hebbels 'Judith.'* Europäische Hochschulschriften, I, 446. Berne, Frankfurt a.M., Las Vegas: Lang.

Walker, Colin. 1981. "Nestroy's *Judith und Holofernes* and Antisemitism in Vienna." *Oxford German Studies* 12: 85-110.

Walla, Friedrich. 1981a. "Über *Prinz Friedrich* von Johann Nestroy. Noch nicht, aber doch schon." *Études Germaniques* 36: 1-14.

Walla, Friedrich. 1981b. "Der Dichter als Handwerker. Selbstzitate bei Nestroy." *Nestroyana* 3: 3-13.

Walla, Friedrich. 1981c. "Von *Einen Jux will er sich machen* bis *Nur keck!*. Johann Nestroy und seine englischen Quellen." *Nestroyana* 3: 33-52.

Yates, W. Edgar. 1981. "Zur Wirklichkeitsbezogenheit der Satire in Nestroys Posse *Eine Wohnung ist zu vermiethen*." *Maske und Kothurn* 27: 147-54.

Ahrens, Helmut. 1982. *Bis zum Lorbeer versteig' ich mich nicht. Johann Nestroy —
sein Leben.* Frankfurt a.M.: Societäts-Verlag.

Berghaus, Günter. 1982. "Quellen zu Nestroys Weltanschauung und Lebensphi-
losophie." *Nestroyana* 4: 3-24.

Breuer, Dieter. 1982. *Geschichte der literarischen Zensur in Deutschland.* Uni-
Taschenbücher, 1208. Heidelberg: Quelle & Meyer. 162-70: "Zensur in
Österreich: Nestroy."

Hüttner, Johann. 1982. "Dokumente zu Nestroys Werk auf der Bühne." *Nestroyana* 4: 54-56.

Koppen, Erwin. 1982. "Die Zeitgenossen Nestroy und Labiche." In *Die österreichische Literatur. Ihr Profil im 19. Jahrhundert (1830-1880)*, ed. Herbert
Zeman. Graz: Akademische Druck- und Verlagsanstalt: 615-32.

Obermaier, Walter. 1982. "Nestroy und seine Freunde." *Nestroyana* 4: 92-97.

Schmidt-Dengler, Wendelin. 1982. "Familienfassaden. Zur Funktion der Familie
bei Johann Nestroy." *Nestroyana* 4: 83-91.

Wimmer, Ruprecht. 1982. "Langue et dramaturgie dans le théâtre de Johann
Nestroy." *Austriaca* (Rouen) 14: 87-102.

Yates, W. E. 1982. "Let's Translate Nestroy." *Forum for Modern Language Studies*
18: 247-57.

Hein, Jürgen. 1983a. "Die Bühne als Welt. Bild und Rolle des Theaters im Werk
Johann Nestroys." *Neue Zürcher Zeitung* 9-10 April 1983 (no. 82): 67-68.

Hein, Jürgen. 1983b. *"Einen Jux will er sich machen."* In *Kleines deutsches Dramen-
lexikon*, ed. Jakob Lehmann: Königstein/Ts.: Athenäum: 253-58.

Yates, W. Edgar. 1983-84. "Kriterien der Nestroyrezeption 1837-1838." *Nestroyana* 5: 3-11.

Obermaier, Walter. 1984. "Johann Nestroys *Häuptling Abendwind* — Offenbachrezeption und satirisches Element." *Nestroyana* 5: 49-58.

Hein, Jürgen. 1984-85. "Der utopische Nestroy." *Nestroyana* 6: 13-23.

Obermaier, Walter. 1984-85. "Neue Einblicke in Nestroys Biographie. I. Die
Gastspielreisen 1834 bis 1836." *Nestroyana* 6: 42-50.

Spohr, Mathias. 1985. "'Man lachte und frug nicht viel, woher und warum'.
Offenbachs Operette *Vent du soir* und Nestroys *Häuptling Abendwind.*" *Neue
Zürcher Zeitung*, 9 November 1985 (no. 261): 68.

Walla, Friedrich. 1985. "Johann Nestroy und der Antisemitismus. Eine Bestand-
aufnahme." *Österreich in Geschichte und Literatur* 29: 37-51.

Yates, W. E. 1985a. "The Idea of the 'Volksstück' in Nestroy's Vienna." *German
Life and Letters* (New Series) 38: 462-73.

Yates, W. E., and John R. P. McKenzie, eds. 1985. *Viennese Popular Theatre. A Symposium — Das Wiener Volkstheater. Ein Symposion.* Exeter: University of Exeter.

Includes:

Berghaus, Günter. 1985. "Rebellion, Reservation, Resignation: Nestroy und die Wiener Gesellschaft 1830-1860." 109-22. (Notes 159-60.)

Hüttner, Johann. 1985. "Der ernste Nestroy." 67-80. (Notes 157.)

McKenzie, John R. P. 1985. "Nestroy's Political Plays." 123-38. (Notes 160-62.)

Obermaier, Walter. 1985. "Nestroy und Ernst Stainhauser." 41-54. (Notes 154-56.)

Rogers, M. A. 1985. "The Servant Problem in Viennese Popular Comedy." 81-92. (Notes 158.)

Yates, W. E. 1985b. "Das Werden eines Nestroystücks." 55-66. (Notes 156-57.)

Yates, W. E. 1985c. "Nestroy, Grillparzer, and the Feminist Cause." 93-107. (Notes 158-59.)

Barker, Andrew W. 1986. "Nestroy and Wittgenstein. Some Thoughts on the Motto to the *Philosophical Investigations.*" *German Life and Letters* (New Series) 39: 161-67.

Valentin, Jean-Marie, ed. 1986. *Volk — Volksstück — Volkstheater im deutschen Sprachraum des 18.-20. Jahrhunderts. Jahrbuch für Internatonale Germanistik,* Series A, vol. 15. Berne: Lang.

Includes:

Hein, Jürgen. 1986. "Zur Funktion der 'musikalischen Einlagen' in den Stücken des Wiener Volkstheaters." 103-26.

Hüttner, Johann. 1986. "Volkstheater als Geschäft: Theaterbetrieb und Publikum im 19. Jahrhundert." 127-49.

Walla, Friedrich. 1986. "Weinberl, Knieriem und Konsorten: Namen kein Schall und Rausch." *Nestroyana* 6: 79-89.

Walter, Klaus-Peter. 1986. "Peter Dickkopf und Mademoiselle de Prosny. Der französische Zeitungsroman *Au Jour le jour* als Vorlage zu *Heimliches Geld, heimliche Liebe.*" *Nestroyana* 6: 90-93.

Wimmer, Ruprecht. 1986. "Der Teufel als Mißverständnis. Gedanken zu Johann Nestroys Posse *Höllenangst* und ihrer französischen Vorlage." *Gallo-Germanica. Wechselwirkungen und Parallelen deutscher und französischer Literatur (18.-20. Jahrhundert),* ed. E. Heftrich and J.-M. Valentin. Nancy: Presses Universitaires de Nancy. 187-205.

Aust, Hugo. 1987. "Nestroy's *Kampl.* Aspekte der klassischen Form." *Wirkendes Wort* 37: 181-92.

Coulson, Anthony S. 1987. "Satiric Metaphor. Individuality and Role in the Comedies of Johann Nestroy." Diss. University of Dublin.

Decker, Craig. 1987. "Towards a Critical *Volksstück*: Nestroy and the Politics of Language." *Monatshefte* 79: 44-61.

Doering, Susan. 1987. "Nestroy und die Zeitgenossen." *Nestroyana* 7: 6-14.

Häusler, Wolfgang. 1987. "Freiheit in Krähwinkel? Biedermeier, Revolution und Reaktion in satirischer Beleuchtung." *Österreich in Geschichte und Literatur* 31: 69-111.

Haida, Peter. 1987. "Nestroy und Heinrich Heine." *Nestroyana* 7: 15-27.

Hein, Jürgen. 1987a. "Nestroys Verhältnis zu den 'Klassikern'." *Neue Zürcher Zeitung.* 17-18 January 1987 (no. 13): 69.

Hein, Jürgen, ed. 1987b. Johann Nestroy. *Höllenangst*. Stuttgart: Reclam.

Hein, Jürgen. 1987c. "Nestroy und die Parodie auf dem Wiener Volkstheater. Mit einem unveröffentlichten Brief Nestroys." *Nestroyana* 7: 41-51.

Hüttner, Johann. 1987. "Zur Konzeption der Ausstellung." In *Von der Bangigkeit des Herzens. Johann Nestroy 125 Jahre tot*. Katalog der Ausstellung im Österreichischen Theatermuseum Mai bis Oktober 1987. Biblos-Schriften, 138. Vienna. 10-64.

Neuber, Wolfgang. 1987. *Nestroys Rhetorik. Wirkungspoetik und Altwiener Volkskomödie im 19. Jahrhundert*. Abhandlungen zur Kunst-, Musik- und Literaturwissenschaft, 373. Bonn: Bouvier.

Obermaier, Walter. 1987. "Nestroyaufführungen in Wien 1938-1945." *Nestroyana* 7: 52-64.

Yates, W. Edgar. 1987. "Nestroy und die Rezensenten." *Nestroyana* 7: 28-40.

Obermaier, Walter. 1988a. "Nestroy-Pflege in Österreich." *Nestroyana* 7: 117-29.

Yates, W. Edgar. 1988a. "Nestroys Weg zur klassischen Posse." *Nestroyana* 7: 93-109.

Aust, Hugo. 1988. "Possendramaturgie des Paares. Zu Nestroys *Mein Freund*." *Nestroyana* 8: 29-38.

Fabry, Joseph. 1988. "Translated and fondly tampered with: Über die Schwierigkeit, Morgenstern, Nestroy und Karl Kraus zu übersetzen." *Wiener Journal*, no. 96, September 1988: 27-28.

Hein, Jürgen. 1988a. "Johann Nestroy: *Der Zerrissene*." In *Komödiensprache. Beiträge zum deutschen Lustspiel zwischen dem 17. und dem 20. Jahrhundert*, ed. Helmut Arntzen. Literatur als Sprache, 5. Münster: Aschendorff. 83-97.

Hein, Jürgen. 1988b. "Judenthematik im Wiener Volkstheater." *Conditio Judaica. Judentum, Antisemitismus und deutschsprachige Literatur vom 18. Jahrhundert bis zum Ersten Weltkrieg*, ed. Hans Otto Horch and Horst Denkler. 2 vols. Tübingen: Niemeyer. 1988-89. 1: 164-86.

Hein, Jürgen. 1988c. [Review of Neuber 1987]. *Germanistik* 29: 186.

Hein, Jürgen. 1988d. "Biedermeiers Glück und Ende. Johann Nestroys *Der böse Geist Lumpazivagabundus.*" In *Deutsche Komödien. Vom Barock bis zur Gegenwart*, ed. Winfried Freund. Uni-Taschenbücher, 1498. Munich: Fink. 97-109.

Münz, Rudolf. 1988. "Nestroy und die Tradition des Volkstheaters." *Impulse* 11: 192-254.

Stroszeck, Hauke. 1988. "Der Millionist und die Milich. Zur Motivik in Johann Nestroys *Der Zerrissene.*" *Nestroyana* 8: 74-85.

Valentin, Jean-Marie, ed. 1988. *Das österreichische Volkstheater im europäischen Zusammenhang 1830-1880*. Berne: Lang.

Includes:

   Doering, Susan. 1988. "Schnipfer oder Dichter? Zur Frage der Vorlagenbearbeitung bei Johann Nestroy." 55-70.

   Obermaier, Walter. 1988b. "Der Einfluß des französischen Theaters auf den Spielplan der Wiener Vorstadtbühnen in den 50er Jahren des 19. Jahrhunderts, insbesondere die Offenbachrezeption Nestroys." 133-53.

   Yates, W. E. 1988b. "'Die Sache hat bereits ein fröhliches Ende erreicht!' Nestroy und das Happy-End." 71-86.

Yates, W. E. 1988c. [Review of Neuber 1987]. *Arbitrium* 6: 293-96.

Adey, Louise. 1989. "'By indirections find directions out': Horváth, Nestroy and the Art of Obliquity." *Sprachkunst* 19 [1988], no. 2 (*Ödön von Horváth zum 50. Todestag*): 107-21.

Aust, Hugo. 1989. "Sprachspiele des Geldes. Ein Nestroysches Thema im Lichte Wittgensteins." *Wirkendes Wort* 39: 357-71.

Häusler, Wolfgang. 1989. "'Überhaupt hat der Fortschritt das an sich, daß er viel größer ausschaut, als er wirklich ist'. Stichworte für den Historiker aus Johann N. Nestroys vorrevolutionärer Posse *Der Schützling* (1847)." *Römische historische Mitteilungen* 31: 419-51.

Hein, Jürgen. 1989a. "Aspekte der Nestroy-Edition." *Editio* 3: 114-24.

Hein, Jürgen. 1989b. "Johann Nestroy." In Hugo Aust, Peter Haida, Jürgen Hein, *Volksstück. Vom Hanswurstspiel zum sozialen Drama der Gegenwart*. Munich: Beck. 143-49.

Spohr, Mathias. 1989. "*Häuptling Abendwind*. Nestroys Entgegnung auf das kulturelle Umfeld der Pariser Operette." *Nestroyana* 9: 17-21.

Walla, Friedrich. 1989. "Johann Nestroy und die Zensur. Krokodil am Geistesstrom oder Die jüngere Schwester der Inquisition." *Nestroyana* 9: 22-34.

Hein, Jürgen. 1989-90. "Frühere Verhältnisse und Alte Bekanntschaften. Eine Berliner Posse als Vorlage eines Nestroy-Stückes." *Nestroyana* 9: 51-59.

Tutschka, Irene T. 1989-90. "Synoptischer Abdruck. *Ein melancholischer Hausknecht — Frühere Verhältnisse.*" *Nestroyana* 9: 61-110.

Bauer, Roger. 1990. "Wienerisches und Europäisches in den Komödien Johann Nepomuk Nestroys." In *Europäische Komödie*, ed. Herbert Mainusch. Darmstadt: Wissenschaftliche Buchgesellschaft. 379-88.

Grimstad, Kari. 1990. "Nestroy in English." In *Momentum dramaticum. Festschrift für Eckehard Catholy*, ed. Linda Dietrick and David G. John. Waterloo, Ontario: University of Waterloo Press. 439-49.

Hein, Jürgen. 1990. *Johann Nestroy*. Sammlung Metzler, 258. Stuttgart: Metzler.

Keith-Smith, Brian, ed. 1990. *Bristol Austrian Studies*. Bristol: University of Bristol.

Includes:

Mills, Ken. 1990. "Alcoholism and the Apocalypse? Reflections on a Norm in Nineteenth-Century Literature. 117-37.

Walker, Colin. 1990. "Nestroy and the Redemptorists." 73-115.

Reese, Joe. 1990. "*Der Zerrissene* and *L'Homme blasé*: A Closer Look at Nestroy's Source." *Modern Austrian Literature* 23, no. 1: 55-67.

Spohr, Mathias, ed. 1990. Jacques Offenbach. *Häuptling Abendwind (Vent du soir)*. Operette in einem Akt von Phillippe Gille. Deutscher Text von Johann Nestroy. Berlin, Wiesbaden: Bote & Bock.

Stroszeck, Hauke. 1990. *Heilsthematik in der Posse. Über Johann Nestroys "Der Talisman."* Aachen: Alano.

Theobald, Rainer. 1990. "Nestroy am Alexanderplatz. Die Berliner Erstaufführung von *Zu ebener Erde und erster Stock.*" *Nestroyana* 10: 55-67.

Yates, W. E. 1990. "Changing Perspectives: The 'doppelte Sexualmoral' in 1841 and 1895. *Das Mädl aus der Vorstadt* and *Liebelei*." In *Erbe und Umbruch in der neueren deutschsprachigen Komödie. Londoner Symposium 1987*, ed. Hanne Castein and Alexander Stillmark. Stuttgarter Arbeiten zur Germanistik, 237. Stuttgart: Heinz. 17-31.

Häusler, Wolfgang. 1991. "'Wart's, Gourmanninen!' Vom Essen und Trinken in Nestroys Possen und in Nestroys Zeit." *Österreich in Geschichte und Literatur* 35: 217-41.

Haida, Peter. 1991. "Von den *Mémoires du Diable* zu den *Papieren des Teufels*. Überlegungen zu Nestroys Umsetzung der französischen Vorlage." *Nestroyana* 11: 43-50.

Hein, Jürgen. 1991a. "Aspekte der Textkonstitution von Nestroys Possen-Szenarien." In *Textkonstitution bei mündlicher und bei schriftlicher Überlieferung*, ed. Martin Stern. Tübingen: Niemeyer. 100-08.

Hein, Jürgen. 1991b. *Das Wiener Volkstheater. Raimund und Nestroy*. Erträge der Forschung, 100. 2nd edn. Darmstadt: Wissenschaftliche Buchgesellschaft.

Hillach, Ansgar. 1991. [Review of Stroszeck 1990]. *Germanistik* 32: 193.

Kaiser, Joachim. 1991. "Vieles ist auf Erden zu thun." Munich, Zürich: Piper. 57-64: "'Lachen sollen d'Leut.' Imaginäres Gespräch mit Johann Nestroy."

Kastl, Maria. 1991. "Beobachtungen zur barocken Predigttradition bei Nestroy." *Jahrbuch der Grillparzer-Gesellschaft*. 3. Folge. 17: 71-83.

McKenzie, John. 1991. "Les Mystères de *Lady und Schneider*: Johann Nestroy und Eugène Sue." *Nestroyana* 11: 51-66.

Schwarz, Egon. 1991. "Thalia in Austria." In *Laughter Unlimited. Essays on Humor, Satire, and the Comic*, ed. Reinhold Grimm and Jost Hermand. Madison, Wisconsin: University of Wisconsin Press. 41-55.

Stieg, Gerald, and Jean-Marie Valentin, eds. 1991. *Johann Nestroy 1801-1862. Vision du monde et écriture dramatique*. Publications de l'Institut d'Allemand d'Asnières, 12. Asnières: Institut d'Allemand d'Asnières (Paris III).

Includes:

Aust, Hugo. 1991. "Einige Überlegungen zum Problem der Literaturnutzung am Beispiel von Eugène Sues *L'Orgueil* und Johann Nestroys *Kampl*." 9-22.

Neuber, Wolfgang. 1991. "Stumme Rhetorik. Sprachlose Wirkungsstrategien in Nestroys Possen *Der Talisman* und *Einen Jux will er sich machen*." 101-08.

Obermaier, Walter. 1991. "Nestroy und die Presse." 109-18

Schneilin, Gérard. 1991. "De *L'Homme blasé* (Duvert et Lauzanne) à *Der Zerrissene* (Nestroy)." 143-56.

Stieg, Gerald. 1991. "Ist Nestroy ein Wiener Dialektdichter?" 157-64.

Valentin, Jean-Marie. 1991. "Nestroy sur la scène française: *Du haut en bas ou Banquiers et fripiers* (Mélesville et Carmouche) et *Zu ebener Erde und erster Stock* (Nestroy)." 177-92.

Yates, W. Edgar. 1991a. "Aus der Werkstatt eines 'schreibelustigen' Genies: Zu Nestroys Bearbeitung englischer Vorlagen." 165-76.

Walla, Fred. 1991. "Johann Nestroy im Urteil und Vorurteil der Kritik." *Österreich in Geschichte und Literatur* 35: 242-62.

Yates, W. Edgar. 1991b. "'So schreiben Sie eine traurige Posse': Ein Zitat im *Talisman* als Scherz für Eingeweihte." *Nestroyana* 11: 84-85.

Adey Huish, Louise. 1992a. "A Source for Nestroy's *Gegen Thorheit giebt es kein Mittel*." *Modern Language Review* 87: 616-25.

Adey Huish, Louise. 1992b. "Zur Geschichte von Nestroys Gastspielen: München berichtet über einen langersehnten Gast." *Nestroyana* 12: 102-15.

Cersowsky, Peter. 1992. *Johann Nestroy oder Nix als philosophische Mussenzen. Eine Einführung*. Uni-Taschenbücher, 1689. Munich: Fink.

Doering, Susan. 1992. *Der wienerische Europäer. Johann Nestroy und die Vorlagen seiner Stücke*. Literatur aus Bayern und Österreich, 5. Munich: W. Ludwig.

Greiner, Bernhard. 1992. *Die Komödie. Eine theatralische Sendung: Grundlagen und Interpretationen*. Tübingen: Francke. 297-310: "Nestroy, *Der Talisman*: Komödie der Vorstadt — die aggressive Entblößung."

Theobald, Rainer. 1992. "'Kolossalstil im Komischen'. Nestroys erstes Prager Gastspiel im Spiegel der Kritik." *Nestroyana* 12: 87-101.

Yates, W. Edgar. 1992. "Nestroy in *Morgenblatt*." *Nestroyana* 12: 81-86.

Häusler, Wolfgang. 1993. "'Die herrliche Gegend zwischen Simmering und Schwechat' — oder: Was hat Nestroy mit Schwechat zu tun?" *Nestroyana* 13: 30-62.

McKenzie, John R. P. 1993. "'Aufgeklärt Occonnelisch, wird Irrland rebellisch.' Political Songs in Nestroy's *Freiheit in Krähwinkel*." In *Connections. Essays in Honour of Eda Sagarra on the Occasion of her 60th Birthday*, ed. Peter Skrine, Rosemary E. Wallbank-Turner, Jonathan West. Stuttgarter Arbeiten zur Germanistik, 281. Stuttgart: Heinz. 169-78.

Theobald, Rainer. 1993. "'Wo Herr Nestroy herabzog, da erhob Raimund.' Die Antipoden des Wiener Volkstheaters im Urteil Carl von Holteis." *Nestroyana* 13: 5-14.

Robertson, Ritchie, and Edward Timms, eds. 1993. *Theatre and Performance in Austria. From Mozart to Jelinek*. Austrian Studies, 4. Edinburgh: Edinburgh University Press.

Includes:

   Adey Huish, Louise, 1993. "Beating the Bounds: Fantasy and Farce in Nestroy's Comedy." 27-38.

   Yates. W. E. 1993a. "Recent Nestroy Scholarship." 158-70.

Yates, W. E. 1993b. "Nestroy in 1847: *Der Schützling* and the Decline of Viennese Popular Theatre." *Modern Language Review* 88: 110-25.

Yates, W. Edgar, ed. 1994. *Vom schaffenden zum edierten Nestroy*. Wiener Vorlesungen: Konversatorien und Studien, 2. Vienna, Munich: Jugend und Volk.

Includes:

   Hein, Jürgen. 1994. "Vom Einfall zum dramatischen Text im Spiegel der Edition." 83-104.

Scheichl, Sigurd Paul. 1994. "Hochdeutsch — Wienerisch — Nestroy. Nestroy und das sprachliche Potential seines Wien." 69-82.

Walla, Friedrich. 1994. "Die Theaterzensur am Beispiel des *Lumpacivagabundus.*" 45-68.

Index

General

Adami, Heinrich 2, 9, 10-11, 83
Adey Huish, Louise 45, 58, 59, 64, 66, 67, 99, 102
Ahrens, Helmut 20, 49, 96
Ambesser, Axel von 36, 38
Angely, Louis 14, 73
Anon. 1, 11, 13, 81, 82, 84
Anzengruber, Ludwig 21-22, 25, 29, 34, 40, 46, 86, 90
Apel, Friedmar 49, 94
Aristophanes 1, 15, 85
Arnold, C. 2, 83
Arnold, K. 4, 9-10, 83
Arnold, Robert F. 28, 87
Arntzen, Helmut 52, 91
Aust, Hugo 54, 58, 59, 60, 65, 69, 70, 79, 97, 98, 99, 101

Bäuerle, Adolf 5, 22, 66
Bahr, Hermann 22-23, 26-27, 86
Balzac, Honoré de 22
Barker, Andrew W. 64, 97
Barlow, John D. 42, 91
Barraclough, Clifford A. 49, 89
Basil, Otto 38, 90
Bauer, Anton 34, 88
Bauer, Roger 38, 51, 54, 63, 70, 90, 93, 100
Bauernfeld, Eduard von 6, 7, 10, 16, 21, 33, 51, 84, 85
Baur, Uwe 51, 64, 95
Berger, Alfred von 18, 22, 27, 38, 86
Berghaus, Günter 53, 65, 66, 93, 96, 97
Besson, Jean-Louis 80
Bietak, Wilhelm 29, 52, 87
Binder, Carl 78
Blasel, Karl 15, 21, 86
Boege, Günther 9, 51, 52, 54, 90
Böhm, Hans 79

Bogner, Wilhelm 3
Boucicault, Dion 34, 64
Branscombe, Peter J. 4, 53, 91, 93
Brecht, Bert 45, 94
Breier, Eduard 9-10, 83
Breuer, Dieter 53, 96
Brill, Siegfried 9, 39, 40, 90
Bruckner, John Peroutka 46, 92
Brukner, Fritz 24, 28, 29, 30, 31, 32, 56, 73, 75, 79, 84
Büchner, Georg 32, 51, 52
Bührmann, Max 32-33, 87
Bujak, Lieselote 29, 52, 88

Canova, Antonio 17
Carl, Karl 6, 8, 9, 11, 12, 21, 30, 31, 57, 84
Carmouche, Pierre-Frédéric-Adolphe 79, 101
Cersowsky, Peter 62, 65-66, 70, 102
Chateaubriand, René 59
Chénier, André 50
Chiavacci, Vincenz 19-20, 29, 78
Chiusano, Italo Alighiero 80
ch l------ 2, 81
Corriher, Kurt 8, 49, 52-53, 94, 95
Costenoble, Carl Ludwig 5, 81
Coulson, Anthony S. 70, 98

Daumier, Honoré 32
Decker, Craig 66, 98
Denkler, Horst 47-48, 52, 91
Destro, Alberto 38, 40, 91
Dickens, Charles 4-5, 54
Diehl, Siegfried 32, 41-42, 52, 90, 91
Dingelstedt, Franz von 2, 12, 81, 82
Doering, Susan 59, 63, 64, 98, 99, 102
Draudt, Manfred 46-47, 94
Dürrenmatt, Friedrich 45
Duvert, Félix-Auguste 101

------e 2, 82
Eder, Alois 49, 54, 91, 92
Eisenreich, Herbert 40, 90
Enzinger, Moriz 27-28, 86
Eörsi, István 80
Esslin, Martin 42, 71, 89

Fabry, Joseph 71, 80, 98
Fischer, Ernst 48, 49, 89
Fontana, Oskar Maurus 34, 36, 88, 89
Forst de Battaglia, Otto 32, 33, 38, 87, 89
Frankl, Ludwig August 4-5, 8, 81
Friedell, Egon 26, 28, 32, 51, 52, 64, 87
Friess, H. 34, 66, 88

Ganghofer, Ludwig 19-20, 29, 78
Gautier, Théophile 5
Gengnagel, Dagmar 38-39, 89
Gille, Philippe 101
Gladt, Karl 19, 20, 28, 31, 90
Glossy, Karl 28, 78
Goethe, Johann Wolfgang von 33, 66
Görgey, Gábor 80
Grabbe, Christian Dietrich 32, 52
Gregor, Joseph 31, 34, 35, 88
Greiner, Bernhard 70, 102
Greiner, Martin 47, 52, 89
Grillparzer, Franz 3, 27, 33, 34, 36, 66, 86, 89
Grimstad, Kari 71, 100
Grois, Louis 4, 21
Gross-Hoffinger, A. J. 7, 81
Grün, Anastasius 51
Gutt, Bernhard 2, 3, 4, 6, 10, 28, 30, 61, 83, 87
Gutzkow, Karl 1, 12, 13-14, 81, 82

Haas, Willy 37-38, 89
Hadamowsky, Franz 31-32, 87, 88
Haeberle, Erwin J. 40, 91
Häusler, Wolfgang 5, 51, 64, 67, 98, 99, 100, 102
Haffner, Karl 31
Haida, Peter 59, 64, 98, 99, 100
Hajnal, Gábor 80
Hamerling, Robert 9, 83
Hannemann, Bruno 52, 53, 72, 93
Harding, Laurence V. 38, 53, 92

Harrison, Robert 80-81
Hebbel, Friedrich 14-15, 18, 24, 28, 52, 62, 67, 84, 85, 89, 91, 95
Hebenstreit, Michael 76, 77
Hein, Jürgen xii, 4, 6, 7, 20, 33, 40-41, 44, 46, 47, 56, 57, 58, 59, 61, 63, 65, 67, 69-70, 71-72, 79, 91, 92, 93, 94, 96, 97, 98, 99, 100, 101, 103
Heine, Heinrich 52, 60, 64, 89, 98
Helmensdorfer, Urs 50, 92
Herles, Helmut 39, 41, 42-43, 53, 66, 90, 92
Herlosssohn, Karl 12, 13, 83
Hillach, Ansgar 39, 41, 43-44, 65, 70, 90, 101
Hilmar, Ernst 53, 91
Hock, Stefan 21-22, 26, 86
Hoffmann, Adolf 28, 29
Hofmannsthal, Hugo von 25
Holl, Theodor 24, 87
Holtei, Karl von 14, 29, 85, 102
Hopp, Friedrich 5, 12
Horváth, Ödön von 45, 64, 100
Hüttner, Johann 9, 16, 34, 47, 51, 53, 54, 56, 57, 60, 63, 64, 69, 79, 83, 90, 92, 93, 94, 95, 96, 97, 98

Jansen, Peter K. 69, 70, 95
Jens, Walter 40, 92

Kahl, Kurt 38, 46, 91
Kaiser, Friedrich 8, 9, 11, 22, 31, 40, 81, 84, 85, 94
Kaiser, Joachim 62, 101
Kalisch, David 78
Kant, Immanuel 40-41
Kastl, Maria 65, 101
Katann, Oskar 33, 87
Keith-Smith, Brian 100
Klotz, Volker 70, 95
Knight, Max 71, 80
Kock, Paul de 58
Körner, Josef 32, 88
Koppen, Erwin 64, 96
Kosch, Wilhelm 22, 86
Kotzebue, August von 40, 93
Kraus, Karl 3, 15, 25-28, 32, 33, 34, 36, 38-39, 40, 41, 44, 45, 46, 72, 79, 80, 86, 87, 95, 98

Kreissler, Félix 80
Kudzus, Winfried 92
Kuh, Emil 15, 16, 18, 24, 85
Kuhn, Christoph 39-40, 90
Kupelwieser, Joseph 42

Labiche, Eugène 64, 96
Laube, Heinrich 16, 85
Lauzanne de Varoussel, Auguste-Thé-
    odore 101
Leiter, Helmut 56
Leixner, Otto von 16, 86
Lewinsky, Ignaz 4, 82
Liebl, Zeno von 35, 88
Liegler, Leopold 24, 26, 27, 30-31, 32,
    48, 51, 87
Lindtberg, Leopold 35, 36
Lipsius, Justus 65-66

McKenzie, John R. P. 49-50, 58-59,
    68-69, 92, 95, 97, 101, 102
März 10, 84
Marggraff, Hermann 12, 13, 83
Markbreiter, M. 2, 83
Matt, Peter von 5, 50-51, 69, 91
Mautner, Franz H. 3, 33-34, 38-39, 41,
    44-46, 47, 61, 62, 68, 70, 72, 79, 87,
    88, 89, 92
May, Erich Joachim 20, 41, 47, 54, 65,
    92
Meisl, Karl 16
Mélesville (Anne-Honoré-Joseph Du-
    veyrier) 79, 101
Mészöly, Dezsö 80
Metternich, Prince Clemens 20, 95
Meyer, Richard M. 15, 24, 86
Mills, Ken 64, 67, 100
Molière 57
Müller, Adolf 57, 73, 74, 75, 76, 77
Müller, Anton 3, 61
Müller, Charles 50
Müller, Gerd 47, 94
Müller-Dietz, Heinz 67, 94
Müllner, Adolf 66
Münz, Rudolf 64, 65, 66, 99

Nadler, Josef 37, 88
Naske, A. C. 4, 81
Necker, Moritz 16, 20-21, 26, 86

Nestroy-Bene, Stephanie 19
Neuber, Wolfgang 12, 47, 64, 65, 94,
    98, 99, 101
Norbert, E. 2, 8, 83
Nordmann, Johannes 9, 82

Obermaier, Walter 3, 17, 35, 36, 47, 56,
    59, 61, 63, 64, 79, 96, 97, 98, 99, 101
Offenbach, Jacques 14, 32, 59, 78, 96,
    99, 101
Ott, Georg 75
Oxenford, John 28

Paryla, Karl 35, 36
Perrot, Jules 32
Pichler, Gustav 73, 78
Plard, Henri 49, 89
Pocar, Ervino 80
Pohl, Emil 58, 100
Pokorny, Franz 12
Poole, John 34
Prätzel, K. G. 58
Preisendanz, Wolfgang 38, 91
Preisner, Rio 20, 47, 48-49, 52, 68, 90,
    91
Pütz, Peter 11, 51, 93

Raimund, Ferdinand 1, 2, 5, 6, 7, 10,
    13, 14, 16, 17, 18-19, 20, 22, 24, 27,
    29, 37, 38, 53, 85, 86, 89, 92, 93, 94,
    101, 102
Raudnitz, L. 10, 83
Raupach, Ernst 32, 70
Reese, Joe 62-63, 100
Reichert, Herbert W. 36, 89
Reimann, Paul 48, 79, 90
Reinhardt, Max 25, 27, 39
Reschauer, Heinrich 16, 85
Robertson, Ritchie 102
Rössler, Helmut 27, 39, 95
Rogers, Michael A. 43-44, 93, 97
Rommel, Otto 3, 4, 24-25, 28, 29, 30-
    31, 32, 33, 36, 37, 38, 40, 41, 44, 46,
    50, 56, 59, 62-63, 79, 87, 88, 89
Roser, Franz 73, 74
Rosner, Leopold 18, 78, 86

Saphir, Moritz Gottlieb 2, 5, 7, 10-11,
    50, 80, 81, 82, 83, 84

Scheck, Ulrich 62, 95
Scheichl, Sigurd Paul 68, 71, 103
Schick, Paul 50, 89
Schiller, Friedrich 14, 40, 66
Schindler, Franz V. 8, 9, 10, 66, 82, 83
Schindler, Otto G. 79
Schlögl, Friedrich 3, 17, 85
Schmidt, Max 6, 8, 81
Schmidt-Dengler, Wendelin 66, 96
Schneilin, Gérard 59, 101
Schnitzler, Arthur 64, 100
Scholz, Wenzel 3, 6, 11, 15, 32, 60
Schwarz, Egon 45, 101
Schwarz, Heinrich 56, 79
Schwarzinger, Heinz 80
Scott, Sir Walter 66
Scutta, Andreas 76
Seeba, Hinrich C. 11, 51-52, 92
Seidlitz, Julius 5, 12, 81
Sengle, Friedrich 39, 46, 52, 64, 95
Shakespeare, William 25, 37, 46-47, 66, 94
Silberstein, August 3, 4, 11, 17, 18, 84
Sittenberger, Hans 21, 22, 27, 86
Slobodkin, G. S. 45, 94
Soulié, Frédéric 58, 97
Soyfer, Jura 34, 88
Speidel, Ludwig 3, 5, 15, 16-17, 85
Spohr, Mathias 59, 96, 99
Stainhauser, Ernst 64
Stenzel, Carl Franz 77
Stieg, Gerald 26, 79, 101
Stierle, Karl-Heinz 49, 93
Stöcklein, Paul 41
Stoessl, Otto 27, 31, 32, 40, 51, 88
Stoppard, Tom 71, 80
Storch, Anton Maria 78
Straube, Emanuel 7, 82
Stroszeck, Hauke 70-71, 99, 100, 101
Sturmbusch, Peter 28, 78
Sue, Eugène 58, 66, 101

Tandori, Dezsö 80
Tewele, Franz 16
Theobald, Rainer 3, 5, 14, 15, 61, 66, 100, 101, 102
Timms, Edward 102
Tönz, Leo 42, 91
Told, F. X. 13

Torberg, Friedrich 36, 90
Trau, Franz 31
Treumann, Carl 31, 32, 60
Tutschka, Irene T. 58, 100
Tuvora, Joseph 6, 66, 81, 82

Urbach, Reinhard 49, 92

Valentin, Jean-Marie 63, 79, 97, 99, 101
Varin, Charles-Victor 59
Viola, József 80
Viola, L. 4, 81
Vischer, Friedrich Theodor 13, 14, 24, 84
Vogl, Johann Nepomuk 8
Volkert, Franz 73

W. 3, 84
Wagner, Dr. 6, 8, 82
Wagner, Richard 15, 85
Walker, Colin 67, 95, 100
Walla, Friedrich 4, 31, 39, 41, 54, 58, 59, 60-61, 62, 63, 65, 67, 68, 69-70, 71, 79, 91, 94, 95, 96, 97, 99, 101, 103
Wallner, Anton 34, 59, 88
Walter, Klaus-Peter 58, 97
Weidmann, Franz Carl 4, 80
Weigel, Hans 25, 35, 36-37, 38, 40, 88, 89, 91
Weisflog, Carl 20
Welch, Sybil and Colin 80
Werner, Richard Maria 18-19, 21, 22, 24, 85
Wiest, Franz 4, 66, 81
Wilder, Thornton 80
Wilson, Katharina 80-81
Wimmer, Ruprecht 51, 59, 96, 97
Windischgrätz, Prince Alfred 49
Wittgenstein, Ludwig 64, 97, 99
Witthauer, Friedrich 6
Wurzbach, Constant von 15, 85

X. Rdl. 11, 84

Yates, W. Edgar 1, 2, 7, 8, 9, 12, 38, 40, 47, 52, 54, 57, 59, 61, 63, 64, 65, 66, 70, 71, 79, 83, 90, 91, 93, 94, 95, 96, 97, 98, 99, 100, 101, 102

Zeidler, Jakob 15, 22, 86
Zerffi, Gustav 57, 59
Zimmel, Karl 56

Nestroy's plays

Die Anverwandten 54, 77, 95

Eisenbahnheiraten 9, 13, 48, 57, 58, 59, 60, 76, 82

Zu ebener Erde und erster Stock 2, 8, 12, 22, 24, 47-48, 52, 53, 75, 79, 80, 100, 101

Der Färber und sein Zwillingsbruder 67, 68, 76, 90, 102

Die Familien Zwirn, Knieriem und Leim 75, 80

Die verhängnisvolle Faschingsnacht 7, 13, 14, 25, 30, 45, 54, 76, 81, 90

Freiheit in Krähwinkel 11, 21, 26, 40, 47, 48, 49-50, 51-52, 67, 68-69, 77, 80, 84, 92, 93, 95, 102

Mein Freund 70, 77, 98

Der böse Geist Lumpacivagabundus 5, 10, 12, 17, 20, 25, 27, 37, 42, 52, 67, 70, 74, 80, 97, 99, 103

Heimliches Geld, heimliche Liebe 58, 78, 97

Das Gewürzkrämer-Kleeblatt 2, 9, 76, 83

Die Gleichheit der Jahre 58, 75

Glück, Mißbrauch und Rückkehr 1, 6, 7, 13, 20, 57, 58, 75, 81

Häuptling Abendwind 28, 59, 78, 96, 99, 100

Das Haus der Temperamente 2, 19, 60, 75, 80, 81

Die beiden Herrn Söhne 9, 20, 45-46, 54, 76

Höllenangst 19, 37, 38, 42, 51, 53, 59, 69, 77, 97

Judith und Holofernes 15, 18, 19, 28, 35, 37, 48, 49-50, 52, 54, 62, 67-68, 77, 80, 89, 91, 92, 95

Einen Jux will er sich machen 2, 3, 6, 20, 27, 28, 31, 41, 48, 49, 58, 59, 60, 61, 66, 67, 70, 71, 76, 80, 82, 90, 95, 96, 97, 101, 102

Kampl 11, 17, 21, 22, 28, 30, 31, 57, 58, 59, 60, 61, 66, 69, 78, 84, 97, 102

Der Kobold 32, 76

Die zusammengestoppelte Komödie 56, 76

Lady und Schneider 19, 52, 58-59, 69, 77, 101

Liebesgeschichten und Heiratssachen 19, 34, 46, 51, 57, 58, 59, 60, 67, 76, 80, 82, 88, 95, 102

Weder Lorbeerbaum noch Bettelstab 7, 14, 17-18, 29, 33, 37, 45, 62, 75

Zwölf Mädchen in Uniform 4, 14, 15, 42, 73

Das Mädl aus der Vorstadt 9, 10, 14, 32, 48, 59, 64, 76, 81, 100

Der alte Mann mit der jungen Frau 19, 28, 29, 48, 50, 68, 77, 80, 92

Moppels Abenteuer 28, 75, 81

Die beiden Nachtwandler 17-18, 19, 24, 27, 34, 62, 75, 79

Nagerl und Handschuh 16, 74

"Nur keck!" 28, 34, 35, 57, 59, 60, 64, 78, 88, 95, 101

Die Papiere des Teufels 9, 50, 59, 76, 100

Prinz Friedrich 27, 29, 41, 56, 69, 73, 95

Nur Ruhe! 13, 60, 76, 82

Der Schützling 2, 4, 6, 8, 9-10, 14-15, 17, 19, 20, 22, 48, 50, 64, 66, 71, 77, 83, 99, 102

Der Talisman 7-8, 9, 33-34, 38, 39, 41, 42-43, 45, 48, 50, 51, 57, 58, 61, 66, 67, 70-71, 76, 80, 81, 88, 89, 92, 94, 95, 101, 102

Tannhäuser 19, 78

Theaterg'schichten 19, 78

Der Tod am Hochzeitstage 41, 43, 45, 69, 73, 80, 94

Gegen Torheit gibt es kein Mittel 7, 49, 52, 58, 59, 67, 76, 102

Der Treulose 63, 69, 75, 94

Der Unbedeutende 2, 9, 10, 11, 17, 20, 22, 28, 34, 48, 54, 77, 83, 90

Frühere Verhältnisse 19, 43, 58, 70, 78, 100

Das Verlobungsfest im Feenreiche 58, 74

Eine Wohnung ist zu vermieten 2, 5, 8, 20, 26, 48, 49, 52, 75, 81, 87, 95

Der konfuse Zauberer 27, 34, 41, 74, 80, 90

Der Zauberer Suphur... 32, 41, 70, 74, 90

Der Zerrissene 3, 9, 10, 13, 17, 22-23, 26, 33, 53, 58, 59, 60, 61, 62-63, 65-66, 70, 76, 80, 82, 84, 87, 94, 98, 99, 100, 101

Der Zettelträger Papp 28, 73